Teenagers
Unlocking Personal Power

Teenagers
Unlocking Personal Power

MIDGE PATZER

Robbie Dean Press   Ann Arbor, MI

Cover Design by John Meszaros

Copyright © 2006

All rights reserved. No part of this book may be reproduced or transmitted in any form or by any means, electronic or mechanical, including photocopying and recording, or by an information retrieval system, without permission in written form by the publisher.

ISBN: 1-88974-49-6

For making purchases on line, visit the online store of MarketingNewAuthors.com— www.MarketingNewAuthors.com

Contents

ACKNOWLEDGMENTS		1
INTRODUCTION		3
1.	PERSONAL POWER	7
2.	BASIC HUMAN NEEDS	21
3.	UNDERSTANDING THE LIFE BOOK OF TEENS	37
4.	SELF-ESTEEM	55
5.	RESPONSIBILITY	71
6.	ANGER	91
7.	SETTING GOALS FOR SUCCESS	103
8.	SUCCESS IS A TEENAGER LOVING LIFE	119

Acknowledgments

I am deeply grateful to the thousands of teenagers who have shared parts of their lives with me. Thank you! Without each and every one of you this book could never have been written. My husband, Allan, your love and support surrounded me. Trevor, my son, your help is special and necessary. Hilary, my daughter, you always lifted my spirits. My sister, Kate Siegrist, you are "the wind beneath my wings." You never tired of offering me ideas, time, humor, and support. I could not have written this book without you. To my sister Saudamini, your knowledge is priceless. Robbie Dean Press and Dr. Fairy Hayes Scott, thank you for giving my book a life. Gayle Mills, thank you for your support. Your constant belief in my book kept me going. Lisa Stelck, thank you for seeing my vision and believing in my purpose. Chris and Elizabeth Day, you are the best. To my early teacher, Janet Dennis, you helped me get started. Finally, I want to thank Constance Dembrowsky, Institute for Affective Skill Development, for sharing her concepts, "Personal and Social Responsibility," which were often used throughout this book.

I also want to acknowledge all the people who supported me and believed in this book: My parents and my entire family, Herbert Allen, Steven Begleiter, Mike Berman, William Boeger, Linda Crosby, Bill Dickenson, Chrissy and Jim Field, Liz Hilton, Lisbeth Giglio, Bob Mitchell, Joyce Harvey-Morgan, Joni Poole, Joyce Pratt, Will Reed, Janet Taggares, Gary Quinn. Thank you.

Midge Patzer

Introduction

On a child's 13th birthday s/he will come out of his/her room and you won't know who the child is and neither will s/he. The child may look like the sweet twelve year-old that went to sleep the night before, but s/he will suddenly be a complete stranger. Welcome to the teenage years.

The teenage years are a powerful and complex time; they are met by teens and adults alike with confusion, misunderstanding, and anxiety. Parents fear the teen years and worry about what will happen to their relationships with their children when they hit "thirteen." Family and friends with grown children look at new parents "knowingly" and say, "Just wait until he/she hits the teens!" The "teenager as stranger to parents" theme runs through innumerable coming-of-age films from *Rebel Without a Cause (1955)* to *Thirteen (2003)*. There are many books on the subject—both fiction and nonfiction—that illustrate various points of view on this complex time.

I am affectionately called "Patzer" by my students; I have raised two children of my own and have been teaching high school for 30 years. For the past ten years, I have taught the class Psychology of Success. One of my students, a recipient of the Presidential Scholar Award, describes this course in her essay, "What teacher has influenced you the most significantly?":

"In Psychology of Success, Patzer teaches her students more than just the elements of success. She teaches students how to take responsibility for their actions. She demonstrates how the powers of forgiveness and acceptance can overcome the power of hate. She helps students find the confidence to believe in themselves and the desire and abilities to achieve their goals. She teaches students that they deserve respect and love, and they should never accept less. The lessons Patzer has taught me

will carry me far into my adult life, and will help me overcome problems in the years to come."

My enthusiasm is unbridled. I love teenagers. I love their energy and being in their company. *Teenagers: Unlocking Personal Power* brings others into the world of loving teenagers through developing and deepening their relationships. In the words of one of my students:

"I always wanted one of those teachers you read about that you remember forever—both because of who they are and what they give you. You are that teacher! I think this class has saved my life!"

Teenagers: Unlocking Personal Power shares my approach to understanding and guiding teens. Although the basis of my philosophy relies on communication skills that are effective in any relationship, I examine these skills and offer insights into the particular complexities of the teen years that create obstacles in the simplest interactions.

Teenagers: Unlocking Personal Power contains case studies that I have collected over my years working with teens and their families. All the names and identifying details have been changed without affecting the integrity of the illustration. In some instances, I have created composites in order to further disguise the identity of the individuals.

My approach *works*. It has worked with thousands of teens over three decades. This approach has been so successful that I have earned the title "Teen Guru" in my community.

A former student shares her feelings about using Personal Power to deal with a crisis:

Ms. Patzer,
I don't know if you remember me, but I took Psychology of Success a few years ago. I just want to tell you how much your class meant to me then and now. I was in a car wreck almost seven weeks ago. I hit a tree. My seatbelt saved my life. My injuries were all pretty minor except for my

brain. Even that damage is expected to be temporary. Remembering what I learned in your class has helped me every day. I even have a list of goals for each day and some more long-term recovery goals. Taking responsibility for all of my choices helps a lot. I work hard every day reading and writing. I am getting better slowly, but even my doctors see improvement. So, however painful and frustrating or even scary it is—it's working. My choice to see it as an opportunity and less as an obstacle has made it better, too. I don't think that I would be in as good of a spot as I am now without your class. You showed me the tools and gave me practice so I could save my hope. Thanks Patzer, I think you saved my life.

Colleagues, parents, and teenagers all notice that I have a "gift" for working with teens. My techniques can be shared and learned and—with practice—can create an environment where teens and the people in their lives can embrace this dynamic time of life with joy, instead of fear and conflict. *Teenagers: Unlocking Personal Power* demystifies my approach and provides moving examples from my years of experience to illustrate clearly my method.

As Melinda, age 17, realized after taking Psychology of Success:

"You know what's cool, Patzer? Now I know what I want to do for a living. I want to be like you. I want to help teenagers help themselves."

One

Personal Power

"I've been so happy lately. I don't know what to make of it. It's really weird. I'm already a happy person, but lately there has been a ton of happiness."

Teens want to succeed. For many years, I've asked my students this question: "How many of you want to succeed in life?" I have never—and I mean never—had a young person tell me that their ultimate goal was failure. How is it possible that so many teens seem headed down that path? The answer is simple: they have not yet discovered how to tap into their Personal Power. Instead, they become entangled in a web of anger and fear that often leads to drugs, alcohol, and other self-destructive behaviors.

Success occurs when teens discover and embrace their PERSONAL POWER. What is Personal Power?

- ◊ Personal Power is the power that comes from within.
- ◊ Personal Power is internal confidence.
- ◊ Personal Power is dignified, respectful, and responsible.

The benefit of Personal Power is:
- ◊ Love of oneself

With the feeling of Personal Power comes the realization that Personal Power is attractive to others.

Lisa walked into the gym to speak with me after lunch.

"*I don't get it, Patzer. I just don't get it.*"

Thirty kids played volleyball on the courts around us while we talked.

"*What don't you get, Lisa?*"

"*I don't get Personal Power. I mean, I'm not sure . . . how do you know when you have Personal Power?*"

I said, "*Lisa, look around this gym. Who do you think has Personal Power?*"

She checked out the volleyball courts, looked me straight in the eye and said, "Paul."

I asked her, "*Why Paul? What makes Paul stand out?*"

Lisa thought for a moment. "I don't know, Paul seems to be comfortable in his own skin and he treats everyone with respect. He seems to like himself, and everyone likes him. He doesn't have anything to prove to people. He just stands strong. He knows who he is."

I looked over at her and said, "*You got it! You understand Personal Power.*"

Teenagers are capable of altering and developing their behaviors and their beliefs in a constructive way. Watching teens find and develop their Personal Power is both a joy and a privilege. The self-esteem and self-awareness that accompany Personal Power are just below the surface in most teens. Every teenager has the capacity to uncover his or her Personal Power.

Personal Power applies to everyone. Although this book focuses on teenagers, developing Personal Power is crucial for all ages. Working with teenagers is a unique experience. Their explosive energy is refreshing. They are excitedly anticipating adulthood; yet, they still want to hold on to the innocence of youth. Teenagers are eager to learn about success and to live life in a powerful manner. They readily take risks and willingly embrace new views on life. I rarely hear a teenager say, "Yes, but. . . ." What I hear is, "Oh, I get it!"

Personal Power is not necessarily an easy path for teens. It can be difficult and challenging, but it is the surest path to self-growth. Teenagers have the ability to develop their own Personal Power. Just as they can learn to skateboard or play the piano, they can learn to replace powerless behaviors with powerful choices. If teenagers feel the need to change something about who they are, what they do, or what they believe, they must be willing to be held accountable for these changes.

Teens can learn to be kind, to be positive, and to be responsible. They can learn to have loving relationships, to understand their anger, and to have friends. Teens can move from a path of self-destruction to a path of hope.

One of the most satisfying moments as a mentor is having a young person run up to me with his/her eyes sparkling and exclaim, "Oh my gosh, Patzer, I did it and it worked! I told my mom that I could earn an A in all three classes and I did it. I'm so proud of myself!"

Change is often uncomfortable, but it is necessary for growth. It can be frightening for teenagers to choose to change their habits or beliefs. Change means transforming a part of us into something new. Change means taking the risk of leaving old behaviors, habits, and perceptions.

I received a call from a concerned mother who was upset that her daughter was spending every lunch period and every free moment alone. The daughter claimed not to have any friends and thought no one liked her. I wasn't certain what the mother was asking me to do to help the situation.

That day during lunch, I went out looking for the daughter. I found her sitting under a tree, alone, reading a book, pretending to be occupied. I introduced myself and invited her to visit me in my office when she had a free moment. I returned to my office to finish some work.

Two minutes later, Karen was standing in my doorway. I explained how her mother had called and expressed concern. Karen burst into tears and told me that she hated school, she hated everyone at the school, she hated her life, and she did not know what to do. I told her how I go for a run every day during lunch hour. I invited her to bring her running shoes and join me. I never thought I'd see her again. The next day she came to my office, asked me to give her two seconds to change, and stated she would be ready to go. We ran together every day for the next three years. She spent every lunch hour with me running and talking. At first, her words just poured out, almost desperately.

Although she was bright and beautiful, Karen had low self-esteem. She had given up on her goals, dreams, and herself. She talked to me about the problems in her life: her divorced parents, her emotionally abusive friends, and her anorexia. She shared the negative, powerless elements of the journey she was traveling. I did not judge her. I did not cry for her. I did not feel sorry for her. I encouraged her to see the powerful way. To turn her life journey around, she would have to take the risk of letting go of her self-perceptions. She thought that her life was worthless, that she was unlovable, not smart enough, and not in control. Gradually, she moved to a place where she could defuse these thoughts and embrace the elements of Personal Power (respect for self and others, self-love and understanding, dignity and responsibility).

I witnessed how Karen gradually, but, determinedly, let go of the negative beliefs and the habits that were holding her back. Slowly she began to trust herself, and her powerless thoughts evolved into powerful, directed ideas and insights.

I saw her begin to make friends. She became less dependent, and her self-confidence blossomed. Her Personal Power transformed her appearance. By senior year, Karen was voted homecoming queen and "best looking" by her peers. She went on to excel in college and later received her master's degree in architecture from an Ivy League university. Her life is on track, she believes in herself. She challenges her dreams; she's powerful and successful.

Over the years, I have found that teens communicate more freely when they are engaged in an activity that lessens the intensity of the encounter. I choose from a variety of activities to help students open up—running, walking, gardening, cooking, or baking. Different activities work for different situations, but there is one thing I avoid at all costs. I do not sit a teen across the table from me for a "talk." The intensity can be more than they are prepared to handle and can lead to a shutdown in communication. If we are engaged in an activity, or, if I am engaged in an activity and they are free to relate to the situation as they feel comfortable, they are more likely to let their thoughts and feelings roll.

Terry spent the summer with our family. His life had been turned upside-down by his parents' separation and the tragic and unexpected death of his sister. He was emotionally distraught; he had no idea how to share his feelings or how to handle his sister's death. He had no idea how to continue his life in a powerful way.

One afternoon, I decided to make cookies. He sat on the kitchen counter, drew up his knees, and began talking. I never looked up. I just kept cooking. I made the occasional comment to let him know that I was listening, but, otherwise, I kept on baking and let Terry talk. When the cookies were done, I didn't want to break the spell, so I immediately began another batch. That summer, my freezer was full of cookies, and Terry started to understand where his life was headed. Years later, his family gave me a cookie sheet in gratitude.

"It's not so much that we're afraid of change, or that we are so in love with the old ways, but it is a place in between that we fear. It's like being between trapezes. It's Linus when his blanket is in the dryer. There's nothing to hold on to."

—Marilyn Ferguson

No one can make a teenager change; the responsibility lies within him/her. You cannot make teenagers alter their behaviors or their beliefs. However, you can encourage change through *invitation*.

I use the word "invitation" to promote choices in teenagers. I encourage them to realize that words of advice, orders, demands, and comments are all invitations that can be accepted or rejected. I use the word "invitation" because it is a concept that is clear and easily understood. Teenagers receive invitations all the time. They understand they have both the power and the right to accept or reject every invitation. Adults, peers, siblings, friends, and strangers often give teens advice and personal opinions about what to think or do. Some

---

Ferguson, Marilyn. "Brainy Quotes." 11 March 2006
< www.brainyquote.com/quotes/m/marilynfer151855.html > .

even *demand* that a teen do something. I teach that all messages are invitations regardless of their presentation. Accepting or rejecting an invitation is always a choice. I also stress that every choice has consequences. I invite teenagers to think carefully about how they choose to respond to an invitation and realize that the consequences of their choices can have lasting effects, both positive and negative.

While grocery shopping, a mother of one of my students stopped to talk.

She told me she had asked her daughter to clean her room. She explained that she expected her daughter to clean her room every Sunday and this was a house rule. The young lady informed her mother that I had taught her in my Psychology of Success class that all messages were invitations and she was allowed to say yes or no to the demand or request. She chose to reject the invitation to clean her room and went out with her friends instead. Her mother was completely baffled, and, while she wanted to support what I was teaching, she had a steadfast rule about clean bedrooms. I explained that her daughter was correct in sharing with her mother that information sent to her was an invitation. However, I stress to my students that every choice has a consequence. If her daughter chooses not to clean her room, she is breaking a house rule, and she has to accept the consequence.

A teen always has the right to make a choice, but must realize that every choice comes with consequences. I also invited the mother to understand that making choices and being responsible for both the choice and the consequence is part of growing and gaining Personal Power. I invite teenagers to make choices that are dignified and respectful to themselves and to the other people involved.

When I invite teenagers to make choices that are consistent with Personal Power, I invite them to:

- Be honest
- Be responsible
- Be respectful of themselves and others
- Consider the consequences of their options before making their choice

I do NOT:

- Tell them what to do
- Judge them

During her freshman year at college, my daughter Hilary was invited to join the World Junior Nordic Ski team. The races were in Austria and the team was set to compete for three weeks. After discussing this opportunity with her college coach, she decided to ski for two weeks in Europe, then, return to Vermont, and ski the rest of the season with her college team. After arriving in Europe, she called to say that she had decided to stay the third week. I talked to her college coach, and he made it clear that he wanted her to come back and fulfill her commitment to the ski team. If she chose to stay in Europe, she would miss the races she needed in order to qualify for the final races in the National Collegiate Athletic Association championships and she would not be able to compete on her college team for the rest of the season. I realized that she had made an important decision without thoroughly considering the consequences. I faxed a letter of invitation to her, which read:

Darling Hilary,

I'm so excited that you are having a good time in Europe. What an experience to ski with the best of the best. I'm not surprised that you would like to spend a third week there. I spoke with your coach last night, and he was concerned about your decision to stay. I also feel concerned, and I invite you to return to Vermont for the following reasons:

- *When you left for Europe, you made a commitment not only to the ski team, but also to your coach, and I invite you to fulfill this commitment.*

- *Missing three weeks of school will challenge you in the classroom. I invite you to consider the consequences of that choice.*

I also understand that you have the right to reject my invitation and choose to stay in Europe and ski the last race. I trust and believe that you will make the choice that works best for you, your coach, and the ski team. Let me know what you decide.

Love,
Mom

Six hours later I received her faxed reply:

Got your letter. Thanks. I will arrive on campus as planned. I heard your invitation and—if it is OK with you—I prefer not to discuss my choice to return. I know I am doing the right thing, but it is hard to leave. I'll call when I'm back in the States.

My love to both you and Dad,
Hilary

I find that the more difficult the decision from the teen's perspective, the less they want to discuss their choice. Once they have made their decision and accepted the responsibility and consequences for it, they oftentimes prefer not to discuss it in detail.

As adults, we are often tempted to continue to process our ideas. A teen rarely wants to listen. It is almost irresistible to share our years of experience, our victories and defeats. Often a teen will shut down and turn you off.

One of my students misbehaved in front of a family friend. I tried to gauge his punishment.

"Are you grounded?"

His reply explained his fears, "No, my mom didn't ground me. It's much worse—she wants to TALK to me!"

There is a fine line between acting as a guide through invitation and giving advice. The closer you are to a teen, the more difficult it may be. The distinction is crucial and can make the difference between teens tapping into their Personal Power and feeling out of control.

When a teenagers are offered an invitation to embrace their Personal Power, they can choose to hold their power. When they hold their power, they remain accountable for their thoughts, words, and actions.

Teenagers need to learn how to make their own choices. We all grow through making choices and taking responsibility for the consequences. When making choices, teens need to consider the following parameters:

◇ Is the choice respectful and dignified for everyone involved?
◇ Is the choice legal?

If the answer to either question is no, then, the choice the teen is making will be powerless and the consequence will be negative. If a teen can honestly answer yes to both questions, the choice is consistent with the elements of Personal Power.

After an invitation is offered to a teenager, s/he may choose to accept or reject it. We all hear invitations through the filter of our own life experiences, and teens are no different. We can't control how our words are heard, but we can consciously choose a communication style that is as clear and objective as possible. A teen may ask me, "What would you do if you were me?" Through asking directly for advice, the teen is attempting to shift responsibility for his/her action onto me. The best response is to say, "I am not you. Let's talk about what you are going to choose to do." At that point, the responsibility shifts back, and it is once again possible to support his/her exploration and help the teen on his/her journey.

There are times when a teen will ask about your own experience when trying to make a choice. Remember to keep the focus on the teen. At times, it may be appropriate to disclose a personal story that relates to the issue, but remember to stay clear about the message.

It is helpful to demonstrate how the concept of invitation works through appropriate examples. As teens grasp the fundamentals, you may have the fulfilling experience of watching them begin to use it in their communication with peers by offering invitations of Personal Power to one another.

During my course, Psychology of Success, Melinda became interested in these conversation skills, listening and invitation.

One morning she charged into my office with her eyes on fire. "Patzer, you'll be SO proud of me. Mary called last night and said she wanted to leave home. I invited her to talk while I listened. After ranting and raving, she seemed to calm down. I invited her to think about the consequences of leaving home. Patzer, I truly didn't tell her what to do. She finally said to me 'Melinda, if I leave home, I'll hurt my mom, and she is the one person who truly supports me. I think I'll just go to bed and see how I feel in the morning.' Then, she said the coolest thing. 'Thanks so much for taking the time to listen and for not telling me what to do. It calmed me down, and I think I'll be OK. Thanks Melinda, you're really my friend.'"

Then Melinda looked at me and said, "You know what's cool, Patzer? Now I know what I want to do for a living. I want to be like you. I want to help teenagers help themselves."

When teens begin to experience their Personal Power, they open up with insight and sensitivity to other teens. They begin to realize how important it is to validate and support one other. As they give, they get back.

After Jane's father passed away, she often struggled with her feelings of loneliness. On one particularly rough day, she entered the classroom with her head down and her shoulders slumped. As Marie sat down at her desk, she looked around and noticed the tears streaming down Jane's cheeks. Impulsively, Marie jumped from her desk and landed in Jane's lap, knocking them both to the floor. As they hit the floor, Marie threw her arms around Jane in a huge bear hug. Jane was lost in a moment of love and support. Both of them had tears in their eyes. The moment brought tears to my eyes and their classmates' as well.

Teens who have embraced their Personal Power feel like they are in control of their own lives. Once a teenager accepts Personal Power, that power continues to grow. When teenagers feel in control of their personal lives, they have the confidence to change and take charge of the future. With this newfound confidence comes the ability to think new thoughts and begin the journey toward personal success.

Through Personal Power, teenagers begin to understand the truth—the truth at the core of who they are. They realize no one else can choose how they will live their lives. They begin to feel how precious life is and they live it with love and power.

What can you do to support Personal Power in teenagers? You can invite them to use their Personal Power and support their changes of behavior and beliefs through your relationship with them. This book offers you a framework to do just that. In the following chapters, we will look closely at the tools to understand and work with teens on their journey toward Personal Power.

Two

Basic Human Needs

"When we first met, my basic needs were all messed up. I had no idea who I was, and I can truly say that I am a better person (to myself and others) because of you."

In my work with teenagers, I have found that an understanding of Maslow's Hierarchy of Needs is critical to the development of Personal Power. In the late 1960s a well-known psychologist, Abraham Maslow, theorized that basic human needs can be arranged in five progressive levels. A person must meet the needs of one level in order to advance to the next. The five levels are:

- ◊ Physiological: food, water, exercise, and sleep.
- ◊ Safety: security, predictability, and consistency.
- ◊ Affiliation: caring, understanding, and listening.
- ◊ Self-esteem: goals, positive feelings, and confidence.
- ◊ Self-actualization: concentration, independence, and self-motivation.

The base of the pyramid is physiological needs. Teenagers must take in sufficient food and drink to meet their nutritional requirements. In addition, bodies require a certain amount of exercise and rest in order to function properly.

When one of the basic physiological needs is unmet, it can become the focus of a teen's world. When teenagers are hungry or tired, their emotional power changes. They become angry or irritated more easily. A good night's sleep can actually change how they see themselves and can alter how they choose to live their lives. Often teenagers may not realize the importance of food and sleep. They may not realize how unfulfilled physiological needs will affect their lives.

Alice is seventeen. She walked into my office and began crying, explaining that she felt like a mess. She couldn't sleep at night and was stressed by how her lack of sleep was affecting her grades and her friendships. When I asked her why she couldn't sleep, she was at first embarrassed and reluctant to explain the reason:

"I know this sounds crazy, but I miss having my mom home at night. We need more money, so she's been working at night as well as during the day. It's just really hard on all three of us—my mom, my sister, and me."

I told Alice I could certainly understand how she missed having her mom home at night, and I needed to understand how that was affecting her sleep.

"The reason I can't sleep is because I have so many more chores to do, because I want to help my mom. I'm also taking care of my little sister. She misses my mom and cries at night. When I finally get to bed, I can't sleep because I'm worried about so many things. When my sister cries, I usually sleep with her, and she kicks and tosses all night. I don't know what to do . . . ."

"Does your mom know you're not sleeping?"

"I don't think so, but I can't tell her because I don't want her to worry. She has enough on her mind."

I asked Alice how I could help her, and she said all she needed right then was someone to talk to. Two weeks later, Alice told me her mom had been able to quit her night job because she was working more hours during the day. I asked her if she were sleeping, and she giggled as she replied, "*Yeah, probably more hours than I need.*"

When basic physiological needs are met, a teenager moves to the next level: safety. To fulfill safety needs, teens must begin to ask themselves, "Who am I?" This basic but complex question can give rise to many different emotions including:

- anger
- the impulse to hide
- fear
- sadness
- exhilaration

Teenagers must feel safe. In my experiences with teens, I have found that they often get stuck at this level. The inability of teenagers to meet their safety needs prevents positive progression.

The major components of the safety level are security, predictability, consistency, and comfort:

- Security—teens need to feel protected in their lives.
- Predictability—teens need to know what is going to happen in their lives.
- Consistency—teens need things to stay the same. Change is difficult.
- Comfort—teens need to know what is expected.

Life is constantly changing. Teens feel safe when things stay the same. Any change can cause a teen to feel unsafe, whether the change is because of family problems, a friend moving, or the thought of leaving for college.

Teens need security. They need a safe haven, both physically and emotionally. When I ask teenagers where they go to feel safe, whether it's their room, their car, or a friend's house, the answer is inevitably a place where they feel accepted for who they are. If teenagers feel accepted by their teachers and peers, they may feel the most secure at school. Security creates safety.

Predictability and consistency are important components in teenagers' lives because they want to know what is going to happen. However, in life one thing we can count on is that things *will* change! Change is hard on many teens. It scares them. We can't keep things the same in a teen's life and probably wouldn't want to if we could. What we can do is support a teen through changes.

As adults, when we view changes as positive, we may forget that change is change and in and of itself may be enough to rock a teen's world. A change may be moving teenagers in a positive, forward direction, but, at the same time, it may be sending them back into their safety needs.

When our new high school building opened, a student wrote how she felt in her journal:

I really miss the old school. I miss the old classrooms and ugly colors and carpet on all the floors. I miss the old smell and low ceilings; it was so cozy. Everybody knew everybody and you always saw your friends in the hall. Now everything is so spread out and huge that I don't see anyone I know and nobody knows me. I know I should be thankful for all the new equipment but I can't help missing the old school. It felt more like home. It had spirit, it had memories, and it had laughter and I want that back.

Another student reflected on his upcoming graduation:

Yesterday I started thinking about graduation. Sometimes I am ready to leave and go to college but sometimes I also get nervous and sad to leave people. Also, just the whole experience of being in high school will be hard to leave at first. I've been in high school so long that I feel safe and loved. I am afraid of being "homesick" and I'm not sure how to handle that feeling. I'm a little scared.

Sometimes it's good to look back and remember all of my memories and times with my friends and even the hard times when we all began to know ourselves and learn who we are. I'm ready to leave, but it will be sad at the same time. It will be hard to say good-bye to everyone who was such a big part of my life in the past years.

Any crisis—a divorce, death, leaving home, relationship problems—can trigger insecurity, therefore, preventing the teen from feeling safe. If he or she has already progressed to a higher level, a crisis can send him/her right back into safety issues. Because crisis situations are not predictable or consistent, they can rock a teen's security. Teens may be frightened because they don't know how to feel or what to do.

A mother sat down across from my desk at the fall parent-teacher conferences, looked me in the eye and said, "Mrs. Patzer, I'm worried about my son's self-esteem. I'm hoping for help."

Steve was in my class, Psychology of Success. Four months prior to parent-teacher conferences, his parents had gone through an angry divorce. The father was living with his girlfriend and her two young children. In his journal, Steve had expressed feelings of abandonment, anger, and loneliness. Steve was trapped in the safety level; his mother was talking about the self-esteem level.

The question Steve's mother asked me was, "*Can you help Steve's self-esteem?*" The answer to that question was, "*Yes, I can help.*" I can invite Steve to be responsible for his own life. I can invite Steve to understand that he's not responsible for his father or for his mother. He's not responsible for the divorce. I can create a safe environment in my classroom. I can choose to be consistent and predictable when Steve is in my classroom. I can choose to listen to what he's experiencing when he needs someone to talk to. I can encourage him to think and act in a positive way.

Can I make Steve do anything? No. Can I remove Steve from the safety level and place him in the self-esteem level? No. Can I be a part of his life while he regains safety in his own world? Yes.

Teens want their lives to be secure, predictable, and consistent. When their lives are safe, they're able to express their Personal Power and gain increased independence. When teenagers are scared, they focus on protecting themselves instead of working through issues that foster personal growth.

When life inevitably brings about change, teenagers worry about what's going to happen and how it will affect their lives. They can choose to act on these feelings in positive or negative ways. They often slip back into the safety level because their security has been threatened and they're scared. When life is not predictable or consistent, their comfort disappears.

Emily stood just inside my office and explained to me that she felt like her life was a mess:

"Sometimes I act mean and tough even though that's not who I am. I don't know why I act that way, but I know it's hurting my relationships with my friends and with my boyfriend. It doesn't feel good, and it isn't who I am—but I can't seem to stop myself."

I invited Emily to figure out what triggers her "tough face." *"Go back and think about when you wear the tough mask so you can recognize what you're feeling when it happens. We all wear different masks that fit different needs, and often we don't even realize when we switch our masks or our actions. It's a self-defense mechanism that can be triggered when we're not in our safety zone."*

"It seems to happen when I meet new people. When I met Randy, I was with a group of friends, and I had that crazy show-off face on. I was having fun and being 'the life of the party.' Now I feel like I have to continue in that role when I'm around him. It's not who I am though. I don't want him to think that's who I am because it's not the truth, but I feel like I'm stuck with the mask."

I invited Emily to come to terms with *who she is*. *"The real you is the best because it's the truth. You can choose to be yourself and not worry how other people see you."*

During this time of uncertainty, teens will make mistakes, and it's important to help them move in a powerful direction. "It's not about how many times you fall down; it is about how many times you get up." All you can ask of yourself is that you get up and move forward to become the best YOU can be! We live in a competitive, intense world. Making mistakes and being human is not a welcome idea in a teenager's life. It can be scary. Teenagers can find that self-forgiveness is a difficult chore. It's powerful for teens to learn about themselves—who they are, and who they want to become. It takes a lifetime to do both.

Once these safety needs are met, teens can progress to the next level: affiliation. Affiliation includes:

- ◊ Caring—we need to care about others, and we need others to care about us.
- ◊ Understanding—we need to see things from different points of view.
- ◊ Listening—we need to hear what others are saying.
- ◊ Expressing ourselves—we need to state our opinions and be understood.

Teenagers require love, and they need to know people care about them. They need to care about each other, and they need to care about themselves. It's amazing how often these feelings go unexpressed.

I asked the students in my Psychology of Success class the following question:

Who has been a loving influence in your life? Whom have you cared about and in return has cared about you?

Kate thought for a few minutes and then smiled as she said, "Nemo."

After listening to her explanation about why her English teacher, Nemo, was a loving influence in her life, I asked her if she had ever shared her feelings with him.

She said she hadn't because she didn't know how he would react to hearing how much he meant to her.

I invited Kate to consider sharing her feelings with Nemo, reminding her that everyone likes to hear how s/he has influenced someone's life in a positive way.

The next day, Kate walked into class and told me she had written Nemo a letter. She handed it to me and said, "*I don't know how Nemo will feel, but I feel great about writing this.*"

Two days later as I was working in my office, the door opened, and Nemo walked in. He looked at me, smiled, and handed me Kate's letter—he had framed it.

Understanding ourselves and others is a critical part of the affiliation level. Through growth and experience, teens realize that people have different perspectives. Personal Power develops when teens embrace different points of view, when they listen to and hear what others have to say and in return are heard and understood. It's essential that teens express their opinions with honesty and responsibility so they can be heard clearly.

I asked my class to write down their beliefs. One student wrote:

I believe in my mother, the most caring person in my life. She's someone who helps me, and I know she'll guide me through both good times and hard times.

I believe in my father. He's a loving parent I turn to for advice. He's willing to teach me and do things for me, but he also lets me learn things on my own.

I believe in my grandma, the most daring 59-year-old I know. I believe in her because she's always been there for me, because we always have fun together, and because she's a strong person.

I believe in my grandpa. He's the strongest person I've ever known—my role model. I believe in him because he speaks his mind and isn't afraid to tell people what he thinks.

I believe in all of my good friends—Jake, Brandon, Pat, Anna, and Dana. I believe in them because they're always by my side; they're not fair-weather friends.

I believe in being a gentleman. How you act reflects on you; being polite and treating people with respect will help you in life.

I believe in honesty. You can do better business if you're honest; people will trust you, and you'll be able to do better because you can be trusted.

I believe in relaxing. We need a little down time in our crazy lives. Relaxing lets your body and mind rest and recuperate; it brings your stress level down.

I believe in being nice—it's the key to making friends and it builds character.

I believe in sports. I'm best at sports, and they're a good way to meet new people and keep me in shape.

I believe in winter. I believe in winter because it's my favorite season.

I believe in the freedom of speech—the most important right anyone has.

This student captured the essence of the affiliation level through his perspective on family, friends, and issues he felt were important. He has a strong sense of what matters to him.

Once the affiliation needs are met, a teenager enters the level of self-esteem. The self-esteem level includes:

Personal talents and skills—teens need to know what they do well;

Goals—teens need to know what they want to accomplish;

Positive Feelings—teens need to feel good about themselves and others;

Confidence—teens need to believe in themselves.

The first two points—knowing what you do well and having pre-determined goals—build self-esteem. Teenagers need a clear vision of their personal talents in order to be capable of building on their strengths. They need to know where they are headed and that there is a plan for them.

A senior in high school stated:

I finally decided that I want to go to a mechanic school next year. I love working on cars and I love engines. I know I'm good at that type of work. I'm excited and can't wait to get started. Such a weight has been lifted off my shoulders.

The third point is embracing positive feelings and understanding that feelings are a choice.

A teenager writes in her journal:

I'm so happy. I don't know what to make of it. It's really weird. I decided I felt better about myself when I was happy, so I decided to be happy.

The fourth point is that teenagers need confidence. They need to believe in themselves.

Another journal entry reads:

I'll make a positive difference in the world. I believe the choices I make are the right ones for me, and I'm happy with where I am today. I'll be successful because I want to be successful.

Confidence allows teenagers to dream and to believe in their goals. I received the following email from a former student who was a freshman in college:

I've finally found my "passion." I've decided what I want to do with the rest of my life. I want to go into human rights, helping people in other countries. I don't know whether it will be through a government position or through starting my own company—I really don't know much about it at all, except that it's absolutely what I want to do. I have the confidence, and I've never felt so strong—or as you would say, "so powerful."

- ◊ Self-esteem develops when teenagers know who they are.
- ◊ Self-esteem develops when teenagers embrace their talents.
- ◊ Self-esteem develops when teenagers choose positive feelings.
- ◊ Self-esteem develops when teenagers believe in themselves.

The top level of Maslow's pyramid is self-actualization. This involves developing tools so teenagers can continue to grow stronger by improving themselves and the lives of those around them. At this level, a teenager develops better concentration and the ability to focus.

This journal entry emphasizes the power of concentration and focus:

I took a two-hour math test today, and it felt like it only lasted five minutes. I was so into the test—time just flew. I'm sure I did well because I stayed so focused.

Self-actualization occurs partly through helping others.

Written in a journal after Christmas vacation:

It's really hard to say if my "journey in life" has a heart or not. It's difficult to analyze myself, but I hope what I do is from my heart. I listen and help people as much as possible. I especially enjoy my neighbor who is older and alone. I visit her several times a week and we seem to enjoy each other. I know I help her a lot, but she helps me even more. I try to think of others before myself. I think I'm lucky.

Self-actualization develops when teenagers understand the concept of giving back. They want the world to be a better place as a result of their personal influence.

A journal entry written after a class discussion on making the world a better place:

I wonder if what I'm doing with my life is making a difference. I hope so—maybe it's in ways I'm not aware of. I have dreams of making a difference; I'm just not sure how to do it. I know I'll figure it out.

The level of self-actualization is related to being self-motivated and gaining independence.

This emphasizes the power of self-motivation:

I set a goal to run twice a week for three months. I have done exactly that. The best part is that no one runs with me. I had never done anything without my friends, and this time I am. I'm so proud of myself. I realize that I can do whatever I want, and I can do it alone.

Reaching the tip of the pyramid involves being persistent and not giving up.

A teenager will find personal power through persistence:

I'll never quit. I'll do it over and over until it works. No one can make me quit. If it takes a lifetime, that's OK—I still won't quit. I'll reach my dreams; I know it will happen.

I tell my class, "The peak of the pyramid, self-actualization, is the home of Mahatma Gandhi and Mother Teresa." When teenagers reach the level of self-actualization, they are focused on bettering themselves and the world. They will find meaning and contentment in both.

Maslow's Hierarchy of Needs helps clarify where teenagers are on their respective journeys. It becomes easy to visualize the journey, one level at a time. To review:

- Physiological: food, water, exercise, and sleep.
- Safety: security, predictability, and consistency.
- Affiliation: caring, understanding, and listening.
- Self-esteem: goals, positive feelings, and confidence.
- Self-actualization: concentration, independence, and self-motivation.

Maslow's Basic Needs are **needs, not wants**. **Needs** must first be met before **wants** are realized. A teenager may *want* to have high self-esteem, but as long as his/her safety needs remain unmet, there's an obstacle to having self-esteem. Teenagers may dream of being self-motivated, but, if they don't have the tools to care about themselves and other people, they'll remain challenged by the affiliation level.

Teenagers' lives are constantly changing and so is their placement on the pyramid. Personal Power invites teenagers to become better and better with each day. Teenagers can always choose to help themselves. Through realizing their Personal Power, all teens will strive to succeed.

It's possible for each and every teenager to reach the level of self-actualization. When the journey appears long and difficult, I remind them of one of my favorite quotes: "How do you eat an elephant? One bite at a time."

Three

Understanding The Life Book of Teens

"Thank you for having an open mind. Thank you for being objective. Thank you for listening without judgment and thank you for helping me discover my Personal Power."

It is a joy to talk with teens when their energy is positive, but how do you reach a teenager whose energy has become negative? The emotions that they grapple with on a daily basis include joy, frustration, happiness, anger, compassion, sadness, and disappointment. They need and want to communicate their feelings and to be understood. The challenge is finding a non-threatening way for them to do this.

How do you encourage a young person to communicate clearly when s/he is spitting venom? There are a number of communication skills that can be learned, practiced, and successfully applied in building relationships with teenagers. For instance, it is particularly vital that you choose and develop a personal communication style that is comfortable for them. Teens are adept at detecting a "false voice." If they feel you are not communicating from your heart, they are likely to close down and go somewhere else for help. One of my favorite sayings is, "No one cares how much you know until they know how much you care."

Teenagers are perceptive about how people see them and how people treat them.

One young man expressed his frustrations by saying:

> It really ticks me off when people use their power against me. Why do people treat me in such weird ways? What do they really think I might do? It gives me a funny feeling inside. I feel like if people treated me with respect and cared about me, I'd be really nice to them. If people just talked to me, then I could share my feelings. Sometimes I feel like people are rude to me just to see if I will react. And do you know what? I *do* react. That's the worst part because it doesn't feel good.

Verbal and nonverbal communication skills—when used appropriately—can be particularly effective with teens. There is no hard and fast rule, but there are a range of approaches that can be adapted to each person's capacity and comfort zone.

Verbal Communication

Words are a powerful way to communicate and can be used to issue an invitation. You cannot control how a teen hears and responds to your invitation, but you can make sure that your communication is clear, calm, and non-threatening. You are in control of what you say and how you say it, but there is no way to control what they hear or how they hear it. This can be tricky, but if you are clear, calm, and non-threatening, your ability to communicate effectively with teenagers will increase immeasurably.

We all interpret the world through the filter of our own personal experiences. Those experiences comprise the "book" of our lives and no two books read alike. Someone with fifteen years of life experience does not respond the same way in the same circumstances as someone with fifty years of life experience. The miracle is that we manage to communicate at all!

Misunderstanding the *intent* of the spoken message is where conversations with teens often go wrong. The volley of messages can quickly spiral out of control and result in a complete breakdown in communication. By paying attention to communication skills, you can help teenagers voice their concerns in a way that gives you enough information to assist them.

The first step is to clarify the issue. What happened? Listen to their story and *how* they tell it. Then clarify the feeling(s). Are they sad, angry, hurt, afraid, confused . . . or is it a combination of these feelings? By listening and asking the right questions, you can begin to understand what teenagers are saying and feeling, instead of what you *perceive* they are saying based on your own experience.

If you want to help teens with a problem, you must *listen* to them. I continually remind myself of the saying, "God gave us two ears and one mouth. Use them in that proportion." What teenagers need are people who will listen—not judge, not give advice—but simply listen to their needs.

You must listen, repeat, listen, and repeat . . . the process is not complicated. You listen carefully to what they say and then you repeat back to them what you heard. At times, the process may seem repetitive. When you repeat their exact words and they hear the words echoed back, they may disagree. If they do, they will let you know, "That is *not* what I said."

It is imperative not to contradict or argue with them; this is a time for patience. Ask them to explain again what was said to help you better understand what they are saying. Say something like, "OK, tell me again." Remember, what a teen said and what s/he *believed* the teen said may not be a perfect match. Listen, repeat, listen, and repeat; this is the key. Once teens agree with what you repeated, they will let you know. Listen to their words, repeat them, and wait for their reaction. At some point, they will say, "Yes, *now* you get it. That *is* what happened, that is what I feel!" When they hear you repeat their own words and feelings, communication has become clear and non-threatening.

Issue: I was walking down the hall to my office and saw Sara sitting on the floor at the end of the corridor. As I approached she looked up, tears running down her cheeks. "Hey Sara, what's the problem? Will you share with me?" Her crying quickly turned to sobbing.

Listen: "Patzer, my boyfriend spent Saturday night with my best friend. I'm so angry."

Repeat: "So you're angry because your boyfriend and best friend spent Saturday night together?"

Listen: "Patzer, I never said they spent the *night* together!"

Clarification: "OK, I misunderstood. When were they together?"

Listen: "They spent the *evening* together when I was out with my family."

Repeat: "So your boyfriend and best friend spent Saturday evening together?"

Confirmation: "Yes, that's what my friends told me."

Clarification: "Are you angry with your best friend? Are you angry with your boyfriend? Where is the anger coming from?"

Listen: "I don't know that I'm really angry. I'm just so hurt."

Clarification: "Did they hurt your feelings?"

Listen: "Yes, they hurt my feelings. I can't believe they were together."

Repeat: "So you're hurt because your boyfriend was with your best friend this weekend?"

Listen: "Yeah, I'm hurt, *and* I'm mad. I would never do that to *her*."

Repeat: "I'm hearing you say that you're hurt and you're also angry. Is that right?"

Confirmation: "Yes, that's right. I'm both those things."

Once the issue and the feelings are clear, move on to the next step—assisting the teen to discover his/her plan of action. In teens' hearts, they may already know what course they are planning to take. They may ask for advice, or they may even ask you to solve their problem. Remember not to attempt to solve their problem, but to listen, repeat, listen, and repeat. This way you can help them discover a way forward, the way that will increase their responsibility and their Personal Power while helping them understand what is truly troubling them.

When you ask teens about their plan of action, they will often redirect the question to you. Remember to avoid the temptation to give advice. If they ask what they should do, don't tell them what to do. Instead, ask them what *they* want to do. This will place the responsibility back on them. They will begin to work through their thoughts and feelings. By helping teens discover their plan of action, you are inviting them to own responsibility for their choices and increasing their Personal Power.

"Sara, what do you want to do?"

"I don't know what I want to do. What do you think I should do?"

"Sara, I'd love to hear what you want to do. What's your plan?"

"I don't know. If I knew what I should do, I wouldn't be sitting here upset. I'd be doing something!"

"Sara, what does your heart say? What do you want to do?"

"Do you think I should break up with my boyfriend?"

"Do you think you should break up with him?"

"Well, I really like him, and I don't know if my boyfriend really did anything wrong."

"So, what do you want to do?"

"Well, I'm really mad at my best friend."

"Sara, what do you want to do?"

"I think I'll write my friend a note telling her exactly how I feel and talk to my boyfriend in person and explain my feelings."

"OK, what I hear you saying is that your plan is to write to your friend explaining your feelings and have a face-to-face conversation with your boyfriend. Is this correct?"

"Yes."

"Do you have a timeline? Are you planning to do this today?"

"I can't talk to him today because he has to go straight to work, and this evening I'm going out to dinner with my family. My plan is to talk to him tomorrow. But I think I'll write the letter to my friend today."

"You think you will or you will? Which is it?"

"I'll write the letter now. I'll feel better after I get my thoughts on paper."

"Sara, I'd like to touch base with you tomorrow. Keep me posted on how things are going."

"Thanks, Patzer. I'll see you tomorrow."

Keep the focus on the teen. When a teenager is working through an issue, s/he is probably not interested in hearing about your experiences. They want to talk about what is happening to them.

For example, a teenager does not want to hear, "When I was your age, the same thing happened to me. I know what you should do." This approach can easily backfire and takes the responsibility away from the teen.

Another typical response is, "You are so young. You have so much of your life ahead of you. Once you have more experience, you'll see what I mean." Based on their years of experience, they know what they feel. If you want to invite teenagers to resolve an issue while maintaining their Personal Power, you must be ready to respect their feelings and their point of view; you must be ready to read their "life book."

Issue: John walked by my desk one afternoon. Looking into his eyes and sensing his energy, I knew he was angry.

"Hey John, what's going on?"

"I'm so mad at my mom."

"Do you want to talk about it?"

"I told her last night that I'd be home by 10:00 and I came home at 11:15. It wasn't my fault because I couldn't get a ride. My friend wanted to wait until the movie was over. When I got home, she was so freaked out that I couldn't talk to her. She kept screaming about how disrespectful and hurtful I am. I'm not disrespectful. I couldn't get a ride home until 11:15. I came home as soon as I could. I think she treated me with disrespect."

"John, did I hear you say you were hurt and angry?"

I'm angry. But I'm also hurt because I don't think she trusts me anymore."

"You think that your mom no longer trusts you?"

"Well, I think she trusts me about a lot of things, but she sure didn't show it last night. She thought I was lying to her."

"Were you?"

"No, I couldn't hook a ride home."

"What I hear you saying is that you're angry, or at least a little angry. You're hurt because your mom has lost trust in you. Is this what you're saying?"

"Yeah, wouldn't you feel the same way?"

"I can't answer that question. It's about you. What are you going to do?"

"I don't know. I'm so mad at her right now. I don't care if I ever see her again."

"Are you willing to remain mad for the rest of your life, or are you looking for a solution?"

"She's my mom and I don't want to be mad at her forever, but her actions were out of control. What would you do?"

"John, let's talk about how *you* feel and what *you* want to do."

"What if I wrote her a note telling her that I was sorry for being late?"

"It's important to be truthful if you want her trust. Do you truly feel sorry?"

"Yes, I feel bad and I know that I *could* talk to her, but I don't think she wants to talk to me."

"OK, so you're going to write to her. What's your time frame?"

"I'll write the note during lunch and give it to her when I get home from school."

When you listen to what teens are saying about their issues and resist telling them what to do, they will begin to discover their plan of action.

If teenager shifts the responsibility and asks you to make the choice for them, put the ball back in their court. By keeping the focus of the conversation on them, you will show that you respect their feelings and point of view. You will also challenge them to come up with the solution.

Issue: During a physical education class, Brad approached me. He wasn't upset, but he had a question.

"Patzer, do you think I should play spring soccer or baseball?"

"That's an interesting question. Why don't you tell me what you're thinking?"

"Well, it's baseball season and that's my sport, but I had such a great time in soccer last fall. I want to play soccer."

"Brad, you've played baseball for so many years—if you choose not to play, will your heart be OK with that decision?"

"I love soccer so much, and I don't think I even like baseball anymore."

"What I hear you saying is that you're considering playing soccer instead of baseball this season because you like soccer better. Is that correct?"

"Yeah, it's hard though because I still like baseball and I'll miss playing and being part of the team. What should I do?"

"Brad, I'm hearing confusion in your voice."

"Yeah, I feel confused. Wouldn't you?"

"Well, I don't play either sport, but I am curious about what you are going to do. Have you discussed this decision with your family?"

"Yeah, they would like me to play baseball, but they will support me regardless of my decision."

"What you are going to do?"

"I'm going to play soccer instead of baseball."

Take home points:

- ◊ Clarify the issue by listening, repeating, listening, and repeating. What happened?
- ◊ Clarify the feeling(s).
- ◊ Choose not to offer advice. Invite teens to uncover their own plan of action.
- ◊ Keep the focus on the teen. Allow him/her time to talk, and listen, listen, listen.

Nonverbal Communication

Teenagers want to be heard but may be afraid of being misunderstood, embarrassed, or judged for their true feelings. Some teens are better at expressing their feelings verbally. Verbal communication may collapse if a teen feels frustrated and unable to explain his/her feelings. This "verbal impasse" frustrates both the teen and the adult. If this happens, a different form of communication, perhaps written, may prove to be more effective.

Written communication can be an effective alternative to direct oral communication and offers a private space where a teen can express his/her thoughts freely. Written communication creates opportunities for teens to explore their feelings and work through their issues on their own at their own pace, which they can then share.

Issue: When my daughter Hilary was fourteen, we struggled to communicate. I found myself desperate for a way to express my feelings. It seemed that whenever we talked, barriers appeared and our conversations often ended in misunderstandings. We needed to find another way to communicate.

I wrote my thoughts, my feelings, and my love in a notebook to Hilary. I put it under her pillow, where I knew she would find it when she was alone. She could choose to read my words when the time felt right. I continued to do this for some time. Whenever I wanted to send another message, I would find the notebook on the floor by her bed, write another entry, and tuck it back under her pillow. I invited her to read my thoughts, but did not request any response. I knew she was reading my thoughts, but she didn't say so and I didn't ask. I had found an avenue to share my feelings and express my love and support.

About a month later, as I climbed into bed, I felt the notebook under *my* pillow. She had written back. As I read her letter, tears ran down my cheeks. We had found a quiet, safe way to communicate. Over the next year, I wrote to her whenever I felt the need to communicate my deepest feelings, and she only wrote back occasionally. Our spoken communication improved as we deepened our understanding of each other. To this day, she has not spoken with me about the notebook. Through writing, our relationship became less stressed, and we gained a greater understanding of each other.

Eight years later, when Hilary read the draft of this book and saw that I had included her story, she smiled her approval.

Teenagers like to receive positive feedback on a daily basis. Writing a short, positive, powerful note on a "sticky note" and placing it in a special spot is an easy way to invite a teenager to communicate, or simply to offer words of encouragement, support, and love.

- ◊ I'm having a "bad hair day." Sorry I lost my temper.
- ◊ I'm glad you're home. My heart is smiling.
- ◊ How was the movie? I missed you.
- ◊ Thanks for listening to me. You're a great kid.
- ◊ Passed your test! Good work.
- ◊ Thanks for helping with the dishes.

When my daughter was a little older, we didn't need to use the notebook anymore, but our written communications continued. I would sometimes scribble a few words on a "Post-it" and place it on her pillow. I was sending her to sleep with the reassurance of my love. Every morning the sticker would appear on her mirror. Before long, her mirror contained hundreds of stickers!

When Hilary was eighteen, two other teenagers came to spend the summer with our family. They were children of family friends, whom Hilary had never met. Steven and Jeannie noticed the stickers on Hilary's mirror and asked her about them. The next morning at breakfast, they asked me why they had not received stickers on their pillows. That night I wrote three stickers:

- ◊ For Hilary: Thanks for being you.
- ◊ For Steven: Our house is your home.
- ◊ For Jeannie: We love having you in our home.

The following night, I found a sticker and four wildflowers on my pillow. The sticker read:

- ◊ Thanks for caring. We love our summer mom.

I fell asleep with a smile on my face.

Written communication is an effective way for teenagers to communicate. When a teenager chooses to put a thought on paper, it becomes more than just a thought, it becomes a *point*.

I have used journals as a teaching aid in Psychology of Success for ten years. We begin every class with a ten-minute journal entry. Each student receives a journal page inviting three responses: something they are thankful for, a success they have experienced, and any other thoughts they wish to express.

Identifying something that they are thankful for invites teens to focus on the positive. The range of responses is endless:

- I am thankful for my mom and dad.
- I am thankful for the mashed potatoes at dinner and the gravy.
- I am thankful for my dog, Henry, even though he slobbers.
- I am thankful for the moon outside my bedroom window.
- I am thankful for my best friend, Sarah.

Identifying a success invites the teen to feel a sense of accomplishment:

- I finished my homework last night.
- I helped my little sister tie her shoes.
- I made all my free throws in the game last night.
- I said "hi" to the boy who always sits alone at lunch.
- I didn't get in a fight with my mom.

Expressing written thoughts gives teens freedom to pour out their heart, without risk of judgment:

- I am a blank slate.
- I have absolutely no method for dealing with the emotional baggage that comes with my problems.
- My mind is going nowhere right now . . . or maybe it's just going too many places too fast for me to tell.
- I have no friends; everyone hates me.
- I am disgusted at how caught up I am in my stupid, silly, pointless, immature drama.
- My head isn't really with my body today. I can't even focus.

◊ One of my biggest struggles is overanalyzing every little detail of every part of my life. I dwell on the past, present, and the future. It's driving me crazy.

I read each journal entry and write a response to the student. Before the next class, I return the page to the student with a new sheet for that day. In this way, I recognize what they have written and acknowledge their thoughts. If teens seem troubled, I invite them to see me privately. More often than not, when they walk into my office, they say, "I *knew* you would want to talk to me once you read my journal." They want to share their problems and experiences with someone who cares. They want to discuss their lives. They often find writing less intimidating than face-to-face conversations.

Often, when I arrive at the door to my classroom, there are kids waiting outside. When they see me, they call out, "Please give me my journal. . . . I have something to tell you!"

Maria ran up to me in the hallway one day and said, "Patzer, Patzer, I can't wait to get to class. Just wait until you read what I'm going to write in my journal today. You won't believe what has happened in my life over the last twenty-four hours. It's crazy."

Writing is a powerful way to communicate with teens, but teenagers also speak with their bodies. They speak with their eyes, facial expressions, and body language.

It is not unusual for their words and body language to contradict each other. They may tell you everything is OK, but the trouble is written on their face.

The first sign of a need to communicate is the failure to make eye contact. Teens do not usually respond well when adults say, "Look at me when I'm speaking to you!" In Psychology of Success, we spend time experiencing the power of "eye language." It's important to understand that, if we choose Personal Power, we are responsible for our nonverbal communication, as well as for our words.

In Psychology of Success class, we engage in nonverbal communication exercises. I randomly divide the students into pairs and invite them to look into their partner's eyes for two minutes. They do not talk, they just look.

"What are we looking for?"

"I want you to read your partner's eyes. What do you think your partner is feeling? What emotions are they expressing through their eyes?" After two minutes, I invite them to write down what they saw and what they felt. I also ask them to write down the color of their partner's eyes.

I paired Lisa and Jimmy. Lisa was a new student in the school. Fifteen seconds into the exercise, Jimmy called out, "Patzer, Lisa won't look at me!" Lisa whispered, "I can't."

After class, I asked Lisa if she had had a hard time with the exercise. She replied, "Yes, it's too personal and I never look in people's eyes." Then, she smiled shyly and said, "His eyes are green."

Before the prom, we discussed the risks associated with inviting someone to the dance. A few days later, we did the "eye" exercise just described. Ellie and Roger were halfway through the two-minute exercise when Roger called out loud enough for the entire class to hear, "Patzer, Ellie likes me. I can see it in her eyes! I think she wants to go to the prom with me!"

Everyone burst out laughing. Ellie and Roger went to the prom together.

What is important in relationships is to recognize nonverbal cues. When you notice the cues, it's helpful to check if something is wrong. It may be as simple as asking, "Is everything OK? I'm here if you want to talk."

When we tune in to teenagers' nonverbal cues, they tell us volumes about what they are experiencing. As teens increase their awareness of the power of nonverbal communication, they are able to use it more effectively themselves in both expressing and receiving information.

Teenagers often ask, "How can you tell that I am not doing well?" "Because," I say, "it's in your eyes."

When Steph walked into my office, I saw anger, sadness, and confusion written all over her face. I realized she needed a safe place to express her feelings.

"Hey, Steph, have you considered taking the Psychology of Success course next semester?"

"Why? What's your class about anyway?"

"My class is about Personal Power, and the reason I ask is because I think you're dealing with some anger and sadness."

"Maybe I am and maybe I'm not, but I was thinking about taking your class when the new semester starts."

The next morning, Steph's father called. After a brief hello, he asked, "Who told you Steph was angry? Did my neighbor call you to gossip about our family life?"

I was shocked. *"No, no one called me. Steph walked into my office, and she seemed angry. I invited her to take my class, Psychology of Success."*

"Steph told me that you wanted her in your class because you thought she had anger issues. I'm curious who told you she was angry because there are people sticking their noses in my business, and I'm sick of it."

"No one told me anything. In fact, I haven't spoken to anyone about Steph. I thought I saw anger in her eyes and on her face. My course focuses on Personal Power, and I thought she might enjoy it."

Regardless of whether a message is sent through verbal or nonverbal communication, the skills remain the same:

1. Clarify the issue. Listen, repeat, listen, repeat.
2. Clarify the feelings.
3. Choose not to offer advice.
4. Keep the focus on the teen.

Four

Self-Esteem

". . . Patzer, you are inspirational. You are motivational. You invite me to be a better person. You have helped me see the truths in life. You are one-of-a-kind. I don't know many people of your caliber and wisdom. This has been my favorite class in high school. Thank you so much."

- ◊ Self-esteem increases as we shift our focus from the external to the INTERNAL.
- ◊ Self-esteem increases when we choose to be POSITIVE.
- ◊ Self-esteem increases when we embrace our personal TALENTS.
- ◊ Self-esteem increases when we understand that it is normal to make MISTAKES.
- ◊ Self-esteem increases when we choose to live with INTEGRITY.

When we are born, the majority of our needs are external; our need to be fed and physically taken care of is of utmost importance. By the time we reach our teenage years, our internal needs increase significantly. Self-esteem develops as the **internal** needs of teenagers are met, and they begin to embrace their internal selves. Whether it is their internal truth, their sense of individuality, their perception of their meaningfulness, or their ability to be self-sufficient, how teens feel and what they believe about themselves will become their jumping off point for their daily choices.

Journal thoughts from teenagers:

"Today's a good day. It's not over yet, but I like the way it's gone so far. I hate living a day just waiting for it to end, and that's why I'm making today a good day."

"Today is a great day. When I look inside myself, I realize I love myself."

"I looked in the mirror and felt ugly. I hate feeling like that. I thought about what I had learned and I shut my eyes, looked inside myself, and thought *maybe I'm not so ugly.* Does that sound crazy?"

As teens gain confidence and self-respect, their self-esteem grows. Teens' self-esteem is externally motivated when peers, parents, siblings, teachers, or outside factors such as grades, clothes, or money control how they see themselves. If teenagers are internally motivated, they take control of their lives and build Personal Power; they're not as susceptible to external influences. Society, however, often invites teenagers to believe that external factors are more important than internal factors:

- ◊ Am I attractive?
- ◊ How much money do I have?
- ◊ What kind of an athlete am I?
- ◊ Do I drive the right car?
- ◊ Do I need to lose weight so people will like me?

When teens are influenced by external factors, it is more difficult for them to focus on their internal selves. However, it's unrealistic to expect any teenager to disregard totally external factors while our society reinforces their value. We can, however, explain that external factors do not build powerful, long-lasting self-esteem. It's important to invite teens to enjoy the external, but embrace the internal. Personal Power and positive self-esteem increase when teenagers choose to value internal factors about themselves.

Not long after graduation, one of my students joined the Army. He left for boot camp in the late summer and just as school began in September, I received the following letter addressed to my Psychology of Success class.

"Here, at boot camp, the only motivation I have is to get through the day intact. The drill sergeants try to keep us motivated, but negative reinforcement isn't enough when you're at your lowest.

"When you're run ragged in your life and you feel like you can't give any more, stay positive and stay powerful. Smiling and laughing keep you going—they recharge your cells. You'll learn a lot in Psychology of Success about life and how to manage your responsibilities. The most important thing I learned was to be open to new things and to believe what my inside tells me. It's really helped me here.

"Remember that motivation comes from within. Your goals and your willpower are not gifts, they come from understanding that what is important cannot be bought. Don't rely on outside sources.

"Take your family and hold them close. Trust me; you'll miss them when you leave."

In my Psychology of Success class, I hand out inspiring quotes, inviting my students to hang them on the mirrors in their bathrooms or bedrooms. An example:

> EVERYTHING CAN BE TAKEN
> FROM A PERSON
> BUT ONE THING.
> WHAT ALONE REMAINS IS
> THE LAST OF HUMAN FREEDOMS,
> THE ABILITY TO CHOOSE ONE'S
> ATTITUDE
> IN A GIVEN SET OF
> CIRCUMSTANCES.
>
> VICTOR FRANKL

When teens are brushing their teeth or hair they tend to read anything in sight, even the tube of toothpaste. If what they read is powerful, it can help promote Personal Power. One of my favorite quotes is taken from a sign on the wall of Shishu Bhavan, the children's home in Calcutta.

ANYWAY

People are unreasonable, illogical, and self-centered,
LOVE THEM ANYWAY
If you do good, people will accuse you of selfish, ulterior motives,
DO GOOD ANYWAY
If you are successful, you win false friends and true enemies,
SUCCEED ANYWAY
The good you do will be forgotten tomorrow,
DO GOOD ANYWAY
Honesty and frankness make you vulnerable,
BE HONEST AND FRANK ANYWAY
What you spent years building may be destroyed overnight,
BUILD ANYWAY
People really need help
but may attack you if you help them,

> HELP PEOPLE ANYWAY
> Give the world the best you have
> and you'll get kicked in the teeth,
> GIVE THE WORLD THE BEST YOU'VE GOT ANYWAY.

Self-esteem increases when teens choose to be **positive**. In any given circumstance, a teenager may choose to be positive or negative. Teenagers, like everyone else, own their feelings and can choose to embrace life feeling powerful and positive, or powerless and negative.

> As one of my students passed me walking into class, she leaned over and shared that she was having a terrible day and felt like her whole life was falling apart. That day, our class talked about attitude, positive feelings, and choices. This is her journal entry from the following day:
>
> *One thing I realized about a bad day is that there is no such thing. And even during a really bad day, it's never really that bad. There are always good things that happen. In a day full of good things where a couple of bad things happen, I consider the day ruined. That's what I did yesterday. Compared to all the things that went right yesterday, it wasn't so bad. I just needed some perspective.*

It's not always easy, but when teenagers choose to focus on the positive, they increase their Personal Power.

> I had one of those precious moments in teaching when I felt like the student instead of the teacher:

One of the assignments in the school's physical education curriculum is to run a trail going up and over the mountain behind the school. Students and teachers have named this run "The Saddle." The trail goes out and around the base of a mountain and then up the backside and down the front side, ending at the back door to the gym of the high school. It's a steep, difficult run.

On a sunny fall day, the class took off and, as usual, twenty-five minutes later students started to cross the finish line. Anna, a heavyset student with little athletic experience, did not appear. When she hadn't returned after fifty minutes, I ran up the front side of the mountain to look for her. I was worried she might have fallen and injured herself. Close to the top, I looked up and saw her. She was on her hands and knees backing down a particularly steep part of the trail. The downhill pitch appeared to make her nervous, but she was not hurt. She hadn't seen me. After considering whether to help or let her finish on her own, I decided to give her the opportunity to complete the run. I turned and retraced my steps to the finish line, staying out of sight but within calling distance from Anna. Twenty-five minutes later, Anna crossed the finish. I expected tears, a confrontation, and possibly a temper fit. I did not expect what happened.

When she crossed the finish line, after seventy-five minutes, Anna looked up and exclaimed, **"I'm so proud of myself! I never knew I could cross a mountain! I can't wait to do it again to see if I can go a little faster!"**

Self-esteem increases when teenagers embrace their **personal talents**. All teenagers are gifted with multiple skills and abilities—their inner "Talents Box." It's important for teens to get to know themselves well enough to recognize each of their special talents. Once they embrace their unique gifts, they can build on them to become the best they can be.

After class, Jennifer asked if I had time to talk. She explained that she was struggling with her position on the basketball team. She seemed angry with the coach and frustrated with herself.

"I think I'm ready to quit. I don't feel like I'm part of the team or a factor in our successes. I don't think the coach likes me because he doesn't ever play me. I'm not that bad!"

I asked Jennifer to take a moment to reach deep inside her heart and, then, tell me how she felt about the game of basketball.

She was quiet for a moment, then said, *"I love the game, but deep down I guess I know I'm not very good. I blame the coach, but I know it's his job to do what's best for the team. Maybe that's part of my frustration. I wish I was better, but I'm not sure I can be. I just wish I could play more because I do love it."*

"What else do you love to do?" I asked her. *"What are your other talents?"*

"I know I'm a good listener. . . . I know I have artistic talent and I know I'm good at helping my little sister with all of her problems, but I love basketball. . . ." Jennifer's eyes lit up as she said, *"I have an idea. . . ."*

A few weeks later, Jennifer took on an after-school project helping girls from the elementary school learn to play basketball.

I invite teenagers to reach inside, open the lid to their "Talents Box," and embrace the positive, powerful, and unique gifts they find there. I share with them the magic of the box—it's always full, yet there's always room for more. By inviting teenagers to recognize their talents and skills, you are inviting them to celebrate who they are and encouraging them to embrace their Personal Power. Positive self-esteem grows from this celebration of self!

After discussing the "Talents Box," teenagers often write in their journals about their skills and abilities:

I have the ability to set goals and the motivation and determination to fulfill my dreams. I have the ability to overcome hardships, put them aside, and go on with my life. Some events, however, have taken longer to recover from and are much more painful.

I'm not really sure what my talents are, but last night I was talking with one of my friends and he told me that I'm one of the most honest people he knows. I thought about that and realized that's one of my talents. I pride myself in being honest; I feel good about that.

I'm very organized and I like that about myself. I also think I learn things easily. I pick stuff up quickly and it doesn't take me long to figure things out.

As teens learn to recognize their talents and skills, they can begin to build on them. As they gain a sense of pride, their self-esteem increases. When teens choose to focus on the external influences, they are less able to embrace fully their talents. Comparing themselves to others can lead to competition and jealousy. Jealousy creates powerlessness.

> I had a problem with jealousy this weekend. My best friend, William, started dating a girl. I felt so left out. I'm used to being the main girl in his life, best friends, and then all of a sudden that changed and he was ignoring me. I was upset all weekend and I'm still upset. I feel mad all the time.

When teens turn their focus inward and fully understand that they are unique and talented, they can build on their own strengths while allowing others to be their best as well.

> There is a lot of musical talent in my family. All of my cousins are talented, yet one cousin seems to get all of the attention. He has a beautiful singing voice and has played the piano most of his life. When we get together as a family, it seems like he is the only one who gets asked to perform. It bothers me and I am jealous of him. I was telling my dad about my feelings and I think he has fixed the problem. At the next family get together my dad organized a talent show and all my cousins were invited to enter. We all sang, played our instruments, and danced. It was a BLAST! Everyone seemed surprised at all the talent and as cousins we had so much fun putting it all together. I am no longer jealous; in fact I am proud to be a part of such a talented family.

Jealousy is frustrating and painful for teens, and, when they choose to be jealous, it's extremely destructive to their self-esteem. When teenagers are able to see clearly, be honest with themselves, and embrace their Personal Power, they are less likely to enter into jealousy.

It is normal to make **mistakes**. Self-esteem increases when teenagers are able to forgive themselves, accept consequences, and move forward.

Andy came into my office with a piece of paper crumbled up in his hand. He was very upset he had received a speeding ticket.

"Were you speeding?" I asked.

"Well, yes, but no one else ever gets a ticket. It just happens to me," he said.

I reminded him that the consequence of speeding is often receiving a speeding ticket.

He told me that he understood, but that it still wasn't fair because the cops never picked on any of his friends, only on him.

I asked him what he planned to do about the ticket.

He told me he would pay the fine, the consequence, that day so that he could move on. Then, he told me he had learned a lesson and would slow down.

Learning from mistakes is an important part of personal growth. If teenagers make mistakes, they need to accept responsibility, correct the error, and, then, be willing to move forward.

Early on a Monday morning, Brandy stopped by my office to share her weekend experiences with me:

"Patzer, on Saturday night, I definitely made powerless choices. My parents thought I was staying overnight at a friend's house, but we planned to spend the night going from party to party. I didn't plan to drink or do anything I shouldn't do. We played pool and I only drank a tiny bit. The bad thing was some kid videotaped the party and I was on tape having a sip of beer. My friend's parents found the tape and said they were going to take it to the school. I was worried to death thinking I was going to be home-schooled for the rest of my life. I talked everything over with my parents and it ends up nothing horrible really happened, but I realize how easily it could have! Man, I made such bad choices. I was lucky! This may sound weird, but I think I learned a lesson I won't repeat."

Teens need to forgive others as well as themselves. Forgiveness is powerful, and it often begins with a commitment to honesty.

During a physical education class, I went running with Dana. She seemed quiet and distant as we began to run, so I asked her if she wanted to talk.

She told her story:

"I told Kathy I'd go over to her house to watch the Super Bowl. She said she was having a party and was excited I was coming. Just before I was supposed to go, a group of my friends called and invited me to a different party. It sounded like a great time and, without another thought, I went to their party. I honestly never thought about Kathy's party again. I guess I assumed she would have plenty of people to have fun with. When I saw Kathy the next day, though, she was upset. She told me that her parents had bought food and drinks for the party. The problem was I was the only friend invited! Her parents were upset, and she cried herself to sleep because she felt like she didn't have any friends. I told her I was sorry, but I don't think it helped."

We kept running in silence.

Finally, she said, "Why don't you say something? It's not really my fault. She should have told me that I was the only one she'd invited."

I continued to run without commenting.

"OK," she said, "I do feel really bad. In fact, I'm not sure what to do. I told her I was sorry and I don't know what else I should do."

"Are you sorry, or are you just saying the words?" I asked.

"I feel *really* horrible. I think I need to ask her to forgive me. I let her down and did it without much thought. I think if I talk to her and really explain how sorry I am, she'll forgive me. I hope so because she's my friend."

Self-esteem increases when teenagers choose to live with **integrity**. Integrity means choosing to have what you think, what you say, and what you do be one and the same. It includes being responsible and trustworthy.

A young man who was having trouble at home wrote me a note:

I think that in all relationships, there needs to be trust. Whether it's between boyfriend and girlfriend, between a child and their parents, or between friends, the relationship doesn't have much meaning and can't function without trust. I've been in situations with friends and with my parents where one of us has broken that trust. I've learned that it takes a lot more than just an apology to rebuild trust. Just saying the words isn't enough; you need to rebuild trust through actions. What I've learned is that, even if it's difficult, you can regain trust if you're sincere and honest.

Saturday night, I told my parents I was going to my friend's house, but I was really with my girlfriend. My parents called my friend's house to tell me they were going to a movie and might not be home when I got back. My friend's mom told my parents that she hadn't seen me all night and, in fact, her son was having dinner with his older brother. My parents were angry and scared. Patzer, I only lied because I believed they wouldn't let me spend time with my girlfriend. I don't think they like her. When I got home, both of my parents were waiting for me. I don't think you can imagine how I felt when I found out how upset they were and that they knew I had lied! I made a mistake; I understand that now. I shouldn't have lied. The truth would have been better.

In our culture, it sometimes seems that people are encouraged to avoid taking responsibility for their actions. To live with integrity, teens must take responsibility for their choices. No matter how it appears, teens don't feel good about themselves when they choose not to live with integrity.

Journal entries from students:

It's easy to write about mistakes I've made and consequences I should have paid. The reason I use the words "should have" is because I rarely pay a consequence. I can almost always get out of trouble. Sometimes I lie, but most of the time I whine until I get my way. I can read your thoughts, "Do you think this is powerful?" My answer is NO, I don't think it's powerful, but I like getting out of trouble.

I wonder what the world would be like if everybody just took responsibility for themselves. Different, I imagine. If people didn't worry so much about what other people did, I think they'd be happier. That's what I'm doing; I'm responsible for my life. Being responsible feels good to me.

Holocaust survivor Elie Wiesel spoke to a group of teenagers. While discussing his memories from the time he spent in the concentration camps, he spoke about integrity:

> THE OPPOSITE OF BEAUTY IS NOT UGLINESS,
> BUT INDIFFERENCE.
>
> THE OPPOSITE OF LOVE IS NOT HATE,
> BUT INDIFFERENCE.
>
> THE OPPOSITE OF KNOWLEDGE IS NOT IGNORANCE,
> BUT INDIFFERENCE.
>
> THE OPPOSITE OF WAR IS NOT PEACE,
> BUT INDIFFERENCE.
>
> THE OPPOSITE OF LIFE IS NOT DEATH,
> BUT INDIFFERENCE.

I encourage teenagers to be **POSITIVE**. I explain that they can choose to be positive even when it's easier to be negative. There is *always* a way to look for what's *right* instead of what's *wrong*.

Teenagers always have choices about how they feel, and every choice has a consequence. Teens can choose their feelings. They can choose to be happy, or they can choose to be sad. They can choose to feel empowered, or they can choose to feel like a victim. No one else has the power to make a teenager feel anything; it's always a choice.

I encourage teenagers to understand their **PERSONAL TALENTS**. Maybe they're a good listener. Or maybe they're gentle. Perhaps, they're good with children. Or, they have a good sense of humor. Every teen has a "Talents Box." The lid just needs to be opened.

When teenagers make **MISTAKES,** I encourage them to accept responsibility, deal with the consequences, and, then, move on.

Teenagers learn through their experiences. If they can learn from a mistake, they are less likely to repeat it.

I encourage all teenagers to live with **INTEGRITY**. To be honest, trustworthy, and dependable is the path to integrity.

In order for teens to realize where integrity begins, it's important for them to recognize that they choose their thoughts, which ones to invest energy in and which ones to let go. Teenagers' thoughts become their words; their words become their actions; their actions turn into their habits; their habits create their character; and their character becomes their future.

How does self-esteem develop? To review:

- ◊ Self-esteem increases through focusing on the INTERNAL.
- ◊ Self-esteem increases through choosing to be POSITIVE.
- ◊ Self-esteem increases through a willingness to embrace personal TALENTS.
- ◊ Self-esteem increases through an understanding of what to do with MISTAKES.
- ◊ Self-esteem increases through choosing to live with INTEGRITY.

Five
Responsibility

> "... You have contributed something very valuable and unique to all three of our children and by so doing, earned our deepest gratitude. We understand that there were times when the kids needed a person they trusted and respected, other than their parents, who would listen and provide honest feedback designed to help them figure out the solution in a responsible manner. You were always the 'go to' person...."

Teenagers are responsible for the following:

- ◊ Their thoughts.
- ◊ Their words.
- ◊ Their actions.

Teenagers' thoughts shape how they see the world. These thoughts create their words and their actions. Teenagers have the ability to consciously transform their thoughts—whether it's from negative to positive, sad to happy, or disheartened to upbeat. If their thoughts are preventing them from reaching their dreams and goals, teenagers can choose to turn those thoughts around in order to move forward powerfully.

Positive thoughts help build Personal Power, while negative thoughts have the potential to destroy Personal Power. It's important for teenagers to understand that they are responsible for making that choice.

Journal reflections from teenagers regarding the power of thoughts:

The way you make things happen and create success is through the thoughts you put in your head. I can be successful at school only if I'm mentally strong. Sometimes we try to blame other people for the way we think, but nobody can control our thoughts except us.

Another teen wrote:

My friend likes to put me down saying hurtful, negative things about my talents, friends, religion, attitude, and family. At first I would feel upset and want to say something mean back but then I started to think about why she was saying those things in the first place. I think she doesn't feel very good about herself. Maybe she doesn't have enough positive strength so she takes it out on me. I decided to change my thoughts and help her instead of being mad. We've had some really long talks and things between us are getting better. I think I can help her gain strength and power by being positive and understanding.

Our thoughts *create* our words. Words are one of the most common ways that we express our thoughts to others. Teenagers own their words and are, therefore, responsible for how they use them. When used with responsibility and honesty, words can be one of the most powerful tools a teen possesses; when used with deceit or blame, words can destroy a teenager's power. It's always a choice—which words to use and how to use them.

> A student in her senior year of high school explained to me:
>
> *Yesterday morning I told my mom I would come home after soccer practice so we could go to a movie. I ended up stopping by my friend's house and didn't get home until 8:30. My mom's feelings were really hurt. I told her I tried to call, but that she didn't answer the phone. I blamed her, and it wasn't even true. I was having fun and just didn't pick up my phone to make the call. I told her how sorry I was, but I didn't choose to be responsible and truthful. Afterwards I felt horrible. Even though I didn't have to face the consequences of what I did, I felt like I had disappointed myself. I made a promise to myself that I will take responsibility to be truthful with my mom if this happens again. I'll take the time to talk to my mom and accept the consequences. It may not always be easy but it will be worth it!*

Teens can use words to support and encourage one other, or they can choose to undermine others through gossip. Gossip is hurtful and can lead to negative consequences for both the sender and the receiver. Unfortunately, awareness of how destructive gossip can be, often comes only through the experience of "being talked about."

Gossip is an important issue for teenagers. When teenagers realize they are responsible for how they use their words and that there are always consequences for the words they choose, they become empowered to make the choice not to gossip.

A teenager wrote in her journal:

Gossip is such a hurtful thing. I've been on both ends when it comes to gossip. I guess when you're saying things about people, you only think about the attention you're getting. You don't think about how it could get back to the person or how it could affect them. But, when you're the person being talked about, it definitely hurts. You can try to tell yourself you don't care what people say or think about you, but it has an effect.

Another teen looks back on the choice he made to gossip:

Have you ever said something negative about someone even when you know they're a good person? You know they're going through hard times and are trying their best, but you still make the comment. I did that, and then I worried about whether or not they'd find out what I said. I just wish I had never said it in the first place.

The temptation to gossip is so strong because teens often think that putting someone else down will make them feel better about themselves. I invite teens to consider whether or not gossiping truly makes them feel better. Does it empower them? What do they feel when they choose to speak those words? How do they feel when someone else chooses to gossip about them? It's important for teens to recognize the effect gossiping has on their Personal Power.

Teens are responsible not only for their words and thoughts, but also for everything they choose to do. They own their actions. Teens may choose to take responsibility for their actions and build Personal Power, or they can blame others for their actions and decrease their Personal Power. Responsibility for their actions is a choice.

A conversation about taking responsibility for choices:

"Patzer, last year I got in trouble and was kicked off the softball team for three weeks. Personally, I don't think my punishment fit the crime. I know the powerless choice I made was having a party when my parents were out of town and they had told me not to. My coach asked about the weekend because he heard about the party. I was honest and admitted to the party, and he said I was GONE for the next three weeks because I had attended a party where there was alcohol. It didn't matter that I had made the choice not to drink. I feel like being honest got me in trouble. It makes me think that honesty isn't always a good thing."

"Were you on an athletic contract that stated you couldn't be at a party where there was alcohol?" I asked.

"Yes, but I told my coach the truth, and that should mean something."

I told my student that I was proud of her for taking responsibility for her actions by telling the truth, and reminded her that she knew what the consequence of being at the party would be.

"Yes, but I don't think it was fair. Everyone else was at the party, and I was the only one kicked off the team."

"The only thing you have control over is yourself. You made the choice to break the rules of the contract, and you paid the consequences. Now you have the choice to learn from your experience and move forward, or to spend your energy focusing on other people."

The more responsible teenagers choose to be, the more Personal Power they will possess, and the more successful their lives will be. It's important for teens to realize that even though it may be difficult to take responsibility when the consequences are unattractive, keeping their integrity has long-term and often immeasurable rewards.

Seven days before high school graduation, Jimmy's English teacher walked into the vice-principal's office and handed him a paper which Jimmy had plagiarized. The teacher told him he would receive a zero and the vice-principal told him he might not be able to graduate.

Jimmy accepted full responsibility, although he did feel that the possibility of not being able to graduate was an overreaction considering he had a 92% in the class.

He went to visit the teacher and apologized for plagiarizing. He asked what he could do to make up for it, admitting that he knew he had made a mistake. He didn't want to be known as a cheater.

The teacher, in turn, also handled the situation with responsibility and power. She explained to Jimmy that the consequence for his choice was a zero on his paper. She, then, offered him the chance to rewrite the paper and receive partial credit. The teacher took the time to let Jimmy know that everyone makes mistakes. She also assured him that she knew he wasn't a cheater by nature and she didn't think less of him as a person.

Jimmy left her office with an opportunity to pay the consequence and rewrite the paper. Moreover, he left with the understanding that even though he had made a mistake, he still held on to his integrity and his power. He spent that evening rewriting the paper and graduated with his class the following week.

Jimmy's mother also handled the situation with responsibility and power. When she received the vice-principal's call, she was stunned, but said, "I'm sorry to hear that Jimmy has jeopardized his graduation, but I think he'll willingly pay the consequence for his actions."

Not long after she spoke to the vice-principal, Jimmy called. "Mom, I realize you're probably upset, and I want you to know that I'm handling everything. I'm rewriting the paper, and I'll walk across the stage on Friday night. I'm sorry. I messed up."

The following morning, Jimmy's mother called and told me what had happened. She said that her heart had stopped at the thought of Jimmy not graduating. She explained, though, that she knew the lesson Jimmy would learn was more important than the act of walking across the stage in a cap and gown. After receiving Jimmy's call, she realized he was a responsible teenager, and instead of anger she began to feel pride.

While it's crucial for teens to accept responsibility for their thoughts, words, and actions, teenagers do not need to take responsibility for what is beyond their control. They often fall into the trap of blaming themselves for things that are out of their hands. They may find themselves taking responsibility for their parents' divorce, their team losing a game, or their friends' problems.

Teenagers need to understand that they are responsible only for themselves. I ask students to stand up and reach out their arms. They are responsible only for what is inside their reach and what is inside their own skin. That's it. Teens are not responsible for their parents, their siblings, or their friends. They should not be held responsible for the choices of others.

Tommy, a high school junior, felt responsible for his parents' divorce.

His mother told him that because he didn't help around the house and take care of his younger brothers and sisters, her stress level was more than she could handle—and that's what had driven his father away. Tommy chose to take those words to heart and blamed himself.

The more he explained to me what was happening, the more he began to understand how big the issues were:

Patzer, it's such a mess, and I have no idea how it got to this point. In my heart, I'd love to help, but I have absolutely no idea how. I keep telling myself that it's not my fault, but I'm honestly not sure. I don't understand my parents' relationship at all. I have a hard enough time just handling my own chores and my own life.

He went on to tell me how busy he was with his personal schedule. He was a capable student, played baseball, and worked as many hours as possible to make the money he needed to cover his own needs.

At the end of the conversation, he said, "I love my parents, but I can't be responsible for their divorce. I don't want to sound selfish, but I think they need to deal with their own problems. I also love my brothers and sisters, but I can't raise them. I think my responsibility is to love my family and be responsible for my own crazy life."

Teenagers shouldn't be held responsible for the actions of their friends. They can offer their friends support, but they're not responsible for their friends' choices.

A student explained her dilemma to me:

I'm in a tough situation. I have a friend whose boyfriend broke up with her. They had been going out for almost two years, and he found out that she had cheated on him. He said he never wanted to see her again.

She was devastated. She stopped eating and she told me that she might not want to live. Her parents found out how upset she was and sent her to a hospital that deals with mental and emotional problems. I don't think she's crazy. I think she just wants to get her ex-boyfriend's attention.

My boyfriend and I went to visit her in the hospital. Patzer, she had this look on her face that I didn't recognize, and she's so skinny. The doctors released her from the hospital, but she's still depressed and I'm worried. Her ex-boyfriend is already together with someone else and she's looking to me for comfort. I don't know what to do. It's so hard to know what to say or what's best for her. I'm afraid for her, and I don't know how to help. I feel so responsible, and I don't want to be involved because it scares me. Please tell me that I'm not responsible.

I assured my student that she was *not* responsible for her friend's actions. I suggested that if she wanted to help her friend, she had the choice to listen without judgment and offer her love and support. I also suggested that she invite her friend to take responsibility for her own life. She could remind her friend that she has the power not only to survive, but to live a full and wonderful life. The most important thing for my student to realize was that, in the end, it was *her friend's* choice.

Accepting responsibility can be a difficult challenge. Teenagers love taking responsibility for the positive events in their lives, yet fear getting into trouble for the negative ones. When teenagers dread the consequences of their actions, they often try to shift the responsibility to someone or something else. George Bernard Shaw sums up responsibility and blame in a quote that states:

> *People are always blaming their circumstances*
> *for what they are.*
> *I don't believe in circumstances.*
> *The people who get on in this world*
> *are the people who get up and look for the circumstances*
> *they want, and, if they can't find them, make them.*

It's common for teenagers to fear taking responsibility for their thoughts, words, and actions. Running from responsibility in order to avoid paying negative consequences, then, becomes the norm.

In a discussion about responsibility and blame, a high school senior made the following comment:

I think I have a hard time comprehending the fact that I'm ultimately responsible for the things I think, do, and say. A lot of the time, I try to blame things on other people or lie about things to make it seem like it's not my fault instead of just saying, 'Yeah, I did it. It was my fault.' Other people may influence me, but deep down I do know I'm responsible for myself and the decisions I make.

Teenagers who deny responsibility tend to blame circumstances on others:

- ◊ The test wasn't fair.
- ◊ My boss is mad at me for no reason.
- ◊ My boyfriend made me stay out late.

Teenagers who accept responsibility take credit for both their successes and their failures:

- ◊ I chose not to study and did poorly on my test.
- ◊ I was late for work and my boss was mad.
- ◊ I was late getting home last night.

Teens do not always see blaming as a powerless choice; they often see it as a survival mechanism. Or they shift responsibility as a way to cope with unwanted consequences and circumstances. It's important for them to recognize that placing blame outside of themselves doesn't change reality. And as long as they continue to place blame outside of themselves, they remain powerless to change a given situation.

Andy walked up to my desk, looked me straight in the eye, and said:

"It's my mom's fault that I'm flunking two of my classes."

"Really?" I asked. "Why do you believe that it's your mother's fault?"

"First, she doesn't wake me up in the morning so that I have time to make my first hour math class. Second, she expects me to do the dishes after dinner, so I don't have time to do my homework."

I responded by asking Andy to think hard about why *he was choosing* not to pass his classes.

Andy took his time answering the question. He shrugged his shoulders, told me he was lazy and tired of homework, grinned, and walked back to his friends. He knew he was ultimately responsible.

Every choice a teenager makes will have an effect on his/her world, then on the worlds of his/her family and friends, and ultimately on the world at large. It's crucial for teenagers to understand that *every choice they make is important.*

I invite teenagers to think about the difference they would like to make in the world. I ask them how they can make the world a better place because they have lived.

Below are comments my students made when I asked them if they were making a positive difference in the world:

"I'm not really making a huge impact on the world, but I do make a positive impact on my community by doing community service and helping other people."

"I'm a caring person, but I don't think what I'm doing right now is making a difference in the world."

"Every day I want to be a positive influence, and almost every day I am. I never know whose life I'm touching, but I know I'm touching lives."

"I remember one time when a girl in class had a birthday and no one was talking to her or wishing her happy birthday. I didn't even know her, but I went up and wished her happy birthday and started talking to her. The feeling was indescribable. I believe it made a difference in the world."

Recognizing and using personal talents is an important part of the journey toward making a positive difference in the world. It is a teenager's responsibility to discover his/her talents and gifts.

I invite teenagers to relive a time when they felt caring, determined, enthusiastic, friendly, gentle, hardworking, helpful, kind or supportive—a time when they were accepting their Personal Power by choosing to use one of their talents.

I ask them to shut their eyes and focus on the emotions, feelings, and thoughts they had while using their gifts. Did they feel internal power? Did they feel good about themselves? I invite them to relive the experience so they can memorize the feeling of Personal Power.

It's important to encourage teenagers to understand that they are responsible for what they create in their lives, both the good and the bad. The thoughts they choose to think and the words they choose to speak create their experiences.

Every thought a teenager thinks directs his/her life in that exact moment. To bring this reality into his/her awareness, I ask my students to write down their last ten thoughts. I then invite them to circle the thoughts that are leading them forward and supporting their Personal Power.

Some of the thoughts students have circled:

- ◊ University of Washington sent me an acceptance letter and now I wonder what I'm going to study.
- ◊ I need to read two chapters of *Hamlet*.
- ◊ Tomorrow I need to look in the local paper and find a job.

Often times, they don't circle any of their thoughts. They appear to be random thoughts, neither positive nor negative. But upon closer inspection, when invited, a teenager can discover that *every* thought is directing his or her life in that given moment.

- ◊ I feel hungry.
- ◊ What should I wear tonight?
- ◊ I hope I don't have much homework.

Teenagers have the power to create their lives. They can decide to be aware of their choices and commit not to let life happen without a plan and goals. Teenagers can be reminded that they have the power to construct their lives, and that this power is so strong that whatever they believe will come true. Teenagers create themselves; they become whatever they believe they are.

I randomly pair my students and invite them to write down five powerful words or phrases that describe their partner. The teenager, after receiving the words, can choose to circle those they agree with. A few examples of what students have written are:

- ◊ Smart
- ◊ Attractive
- ◊ Quiet
- ◊ Funny
- ◊ Friendly

It's powerful to see how a teenager reacts to someone else expressing his or her strengths. It's easy for teenagers to imagine their faults and weaknesses. This exercise invites teenagers to see their talents and strengths from a different perspective.

One way to encourage teenagers to accept responsibility is by emphasizing the importance of internal control over external control. Internal control is when a teenager decides what to think, say, and do. External control is when teenagers allow others to decide what they think, say, and do. Here are two examples:

- INTERNAL—I have so much math homework tonight that I'm choosing not to join Anna for the 7:00 movie.
- EXTERNAL—I promised Anna I would go to the movie tonight, so I'm going even though I should do my math homework.

Peer pressure invites stress into a teenager's life. Having friends and feeling accepted are strong influences on teenagers; those motivations are often the reason for choices they make. Respecting and understanding their need for friends, yet inviting them to take responsibility for their actions can clarify this confusion. Questions that can be asked to invite success:

- What is your heart telling you to do?
- What do you think is the right choice?
- Will this decision make you feel good?

Success in life is largely dependent on a teenager's ability to keep commitments. In order to keep a commitment, a teen must accept responsibility for what s/he thinks, says, and does. Accepting responsibility and not blaming others invites success.

> Megan told me that her history teacher gave her a D in her class. I asked her to rephrase the statement, taking responsibility for the D. She then said, "I received a D in history because I flunked the second test and chose not to bother with the re-take test."

Teenagers can be taught how to speak with responsibility. Statements that are evidence of an acceptance of responsibility start with the word "I."

- ◊ I didn't do my homework.
- ◊ I was mad at my coach.
- ◊ I support my friend by listening to her.
- ◊ I choose to be happy.

Statements that are evidence of a denial of responsibility and a placement of blame start with **"It," someone's name,** or **a pronoun other than "I."**

- ◊ You made me lose my homework.
- ◊ She didn't get me up on time.
- ◊ Dan made me mad in math class.
- ◊ It's not my fault that I am tired; it's Sam's.
- ◊ Harry started the argument; it wasn't my fault.

When teenagers choose to speak responsibly, starting their sentence with "I," they do not blame anything or anyone else. In doing so, they claim their Personal Power.

I encourage parents, as well, to start their sentences with the word **"I."** The word **"you"** invites blame.

When Terry got home an hour late, he was greeted with the following words from his mother:

"**You** have no respect for me. If **you** did, **you** would have called and told me where **you** were. **You** ruined my night's sleep, and **you** make me so mad. **You**'ll pay tomorrow."

> Terry reacted by saying, "I hate hearing **you** yell at me. I'm old enough to take care of myself, so why don't **you** leave me alone?"

The word "you" may unnecessarily push anger buttons. Terry's mother could have chosen to say, "I was worried about you, and I had a hard time sleeping. I'd feel better if I knew you were safe. Is there any way we could agree on a phone call?" Terry likely would have responded in a way that claimed his Personal Power because his mother would have been taking responsibility for how she was feeling and allowing Terry to explain himself without feeling threatened.

Personal Power is built through interactions with other people. When teenagers interact with other people, they're sending them messages in the form of words, expressions, and gestures. Teens are responsible for the message they send and how they send it. How the message is received and what the other person sends back is not their responsibility. How someone chooses to interpret a teenager's message is that person's responsibility.

You cannot do what you do not know. Teenagers make decisions based on what they know. Teenagers who learn the skills of Personal Power are able to apply them and make choices that maintain their personal integrity and show respect for others. Teenagers learn that they, themselves, are responsible for their feelings. They also learn that what they say and do affect others and will, in turn, have an impact on them in return. They learn through this experience to take responsibility for their actions.

> During a class discussion on responsibility and choices, we were talking about feelings. I said, *"No one can make you feel anything. It's your choice. Can someone else make you happy? Can someone else make you mad? Who decides?"*

The next morning one of my students, Billy, burst into my office and said:

"What you talked about in class yesterday doesn't work! Last night I got into an argument with my father and he got really angry. He said, 'You make me so mad! You're making my life miserable!' I looked him in the eye and said, 'I can't make you anything dad; you're responsible for your feelings.' He totally flipped out! See! What you told us doesn't work!"

I had a hard time not laughing when I pictured the scene.

I said, "Billy, you invited your father to become angry, and he accepted your invitation! Remember that you cannot do what you do not know. Understanding that your feelings are your responsibility and that 'no one can make you anything' may be a Personal Power tool that your father doesn't know." I reminded Billy that the heat of battle probably wasn't the best time to let his father know that we're all in control of our own feelings!

A few months later, I ran into Billy's father at a social gathering. Billy had just started his freshman year at college. His father said Billy was doing well and told me about the positive impact the Psychology of Success class had had on Billy. He recalled the earlier incident and started to laugh as he said, "Even that night I knew Billy was right, but I sure wasn't in the mood to hear it!"

How messages are sent and how they are received depends on life experiences. Each of us understands and interprets the world differently according to what we have experienced in our lives. Therefore, words take on different meanings to different people.

Adults interpret through *their* experiences, and teens interpret through *theirs*. Those experiences aren't the same. This doesn't make one of us right and the other wrong; it's often just a problem of communication.

When we talk to teenagers, we expect them to hear what *we* heard ourselves saying. But sometimes that's not what they hear. A parent may say, "Please be home by 11:00 so we can all get a good rest tonight." What a teen may hear is, "Be home earlier than all of your friends so I can sleep. I don't trust you to be out of the house after my bedtime." Teens don't always hear what parents say, and often parents don't understand why teens have such angry responses. It is their choice to hear what they do, but recognizing how we each come to words from different perspectives can lead to communication that produces harmony between teens and parents.

What are you responsible for?

- ◊ The message you send.
- ◊ How you send this message.
- ◊ How you interpret a message sent to you.
- ◊ How you react to a message sent to you.
- ◊ The message you send back.

What is the other person responsible for?

- ◊ Their interpretation of the message you send.
- ◊ How they react to the message you send.
- ◊ The message they send back to you.

I invite students to hold their power in every conversation. I encourage them to choose not to take power from others and not to give away their own power. If there is a question about what you are hearing, it is your responsibility to ask the person to clarify his or her message, explaining your interpretation.

Taking responsibility, whether it is for thoughts, words, or actions, may seem daunting to teenagers at first. As soon as they realize how empowering it is to accept responsibility, however, teenagers are far more likely to do so. Teenagers are responsible for:

- ◊ What they think.
- ◊ What they say.
- ◊ What they do.

Six

Anger

"Yesterday was a bad day. I was mad at myself and mad at the world. I just don't know why."

Have you ever been angry? I have asked thousands of teenagers this question over the past thirty years. I have never had teenagers *not* raise their hand. In fact, the teens often wave their arms and shake their heads up and down as fast as possible to let me know that anger is a daily issue in their lives.

What happens physically and mentally to teenagers when they become angry? What are the feelings or emotions behind anger? What are some coping mechanisms they employ to manage successfully their anger?

Anger is a complex human emotion. By asking a few basic questions, teens can explore what they understand about their own anger. Their responses are a great jumping-off point for discussion, leading to increased self-awareness, Personal Power, and choice. I am frequently impressed by how much insight teens have about their anger. They share these insights with me through individual and group discussions, their journals, and e-mail. Over the years, I have noticed some common responses:

How do you know when you are angry?

- ◊ I start to cry.
- ◊ I shake.

- ◊ I start yelling things that I don't really mean.
- ◊ I feel like hitting someone or something.
- ◊ I stop thinking straight.

What kinds of words and actions cause you to become angry?

- ◊ I get angry when people blame me for things.
- ◊ I get angry when people are mean or lie.
- ◊ I get angry when my feelings are hurt.
- ◊ I get angry easier when I'm tired or hungry.

Do you get angry quickly or does it take a lot for you to become angry?

- ◊ I get angry quickly because I think I'm always a little bit angry. Sometimes, I feel like I'm looking for reasons to be angry.
- ◊ It takes a lot to make me angry. But when I do, I stay that way forever.

How do you feel when you are angry?

- ◊ I feel like I am going to throw up because my stomach is so upset.
- ◊ I get a headache and sometimes I shake.
- ◊ I get sweaty and my face turns red.
- ◊ I feel like I'm going to explode.
- ◊ I get scared because I don't know what to do.

What do you do when you feel angry?

- ◊ I go to my room, lock my door, and cry.
- ◊ I punch the wall or my door.
- ◊ I scream terrible things.
- ◊ I drive as fast as I can.
- ◊ I get in fights.

How does anger affect your relationships?

- ◇ It wrecks relationships.
- ◇ No one wants to be around me.
- ◇ I have a hard time letting my anger go, so the anger stays and the relationship goes.

Sara was describing her responses to feeling angry. She shared that her responses varied depending on the situation.

"Sometimes, I freak out when I'm angry and other times I just get quiet."

I asked, *"Why? What's the difference in your feelings?"*

Her explanation didn't really clear things up. "Sometimes I'm just angrier than other times."

The degree of anger can depend on the intensity of the situation. A teen may be simply displeased or upset. Other times s/he explodes with anger. Teens may become furious. Sometimes, they rage. Regardless of the degree of anger, there are physical changes that affect how they feel.

- ◇ Their pulse rate increases.
- ◇ Their blood pressure increases.
- ◇ Their breathing becomes faster.
- ◇ Their muscles tighten and they feel like striking out.
- ◇ They do not think clearly.

In order to graduate from high school, Joe needed to pass a spelling correspondence course. Two weeks before the course deadline and the date of graduation, Joe finished the class and sent for his final exam. The exam arrived through overnight mail. Joe chose to take the exam in his government teacher's classroom. When the results arrived, Joe did not receive a passing grade. Additionally, the proctor suspected that Joe had used a small spell-checker during his exam. The proctor went to the counselor to discuss Joe's conduct. When they approached him with their suspicions, Joe denied the accusations. He had only two more chances to pass this exam and receive the credit he needed to graduate. Time was running out.

The second time he took the exam, he was asked to sit in the counselors' office under close supervision. Joe was angry and felt misunderstood because he denied cheating on the first exam. At one point, he yelled out, "*If I cheated—then, why did I flunk?*"

Spelling was difficult for Joe. As the exam progressed, he became flustered. He was angry about the cheating allegations. He was angry because he had flunked the first exam, and he was angry because, in order to take the second exam, he had to stay after school and miss work.

Joe expressed his anger in an aggressive, loud, and forceful manner. He felt they were treating him unfairly. As his feelings of anger grew, he became less capable of thinking and taking the exam. His muscles tightened, and he pulled his shoulders up around his ears. In between his angry, rude comments, he was breathing hard and shaking. More than anything, he was not thinking clearly. Under these conditions, it was unlikely that Joe would pass the second exam.

The counselors tried to calm him down, but Joe continued to express his anger verbally. The principal was called in to assist, but Joe was not willing to listen to anyone by then. He was allowed to complete the exam in his agitated state, but he left feeling frustrated knowing inside that he had not done well.

The next morning, Joe and I happened to arrive at school at the same time. We walked into the building together. I took one look at his face and knew he was troubled and enraged. His muscles were tight, his shoulders high, and his eyes were flashing anger.

Joe had taken my Psychology of Success class the previous year, and we had remained in frequent contact. We often saw each other in the halls and always took time to visit. I found his sense of humor endearing, and I sensed he felt safe when talking with me.

When he was troubled, he often wandered into my classroom to talk. I always felt that our relationship had remained positive and powerful. We shared a mutual respect, and I knew Joe trusted me. He knew that I was not going to judge him. He also knew that I would listen to what he had to say and invite him to take the powerful path.

Sensing his distress, I asked if something were troubling him. He explained how he needed to pass the spelling correspondence course to graduate. I was concerned. After twelve years of hard work and receiving passing grades, Joe had put in the necessary effort to graduate. Failure to graduate would have destroyed his confidence and self-esteem. I sensed he was fearful, hurt, and feeling unsupported, and he was not handling the situation in a powerful manner. Joe told me that he was ready to give up and forgo graduation, his way of "showing the school." We walked around the halls talking about his decision not to graduate, and I asked if he had any other options. He said that he could send for the third and final copy of the exam and attempt to pass. He didn't want to take the test in the counselors' office because he was afraid that he would get angry with the counselors again. We discussed the need to take the exam in a quiet, safe environment, and I offered to proctor the exam in my office.

Through our prior relationship, I knew he felt safe around me, and I had complete confidence that Joe would be capable of passing his exam. When it came time to take the test, I invited Joe into my office. I worked quietly while he took the exam. Whenever I noticed tension in his body, I would invite him to place his pencil on the table and take a few deep, slow breaths to calm himself down.

He finished the exam, checked his answers, gave me a high-five, and walked out of my office. I mailed the test to the exam center.

Later that week, the center called with the results. Joe had earned a B on the exam and would graduate with his class. His smile was my reward. He had chosen to be respectful to me and to take responsibility for his actions, which resulted in a passing mark.

Once again, I could feel his internal confidence. Joe had accomplished his goal of completing the spelling correspondence course and graduating with his class. Joe was feeling a sense of peace that comes from successfully taking control of his life.

Anger

Anger is a response to a series of emotions and needs. It may feel as if anger is an immediate response ("When she said that to me, I just saw red!"), but, when teens gain insight into the layers of emotion that lead to seeing red, they discover they have a choice. They *always* have the choice to own their anger and maintain their Personal Power.

- ◊ When you are angry, you are hurt. You might be let down, disappointed, or sad. The question is, why do you feel hurt?
- ◊ You feel hurt because there is something you fear. You might be nervous or worried about something. You might even be petrified. Why is it that you feel fear?
- ◊ You feel fear because there is something you want or something you desire. Why do you want it so badly?
- ◊ You want it because you care. You may care a little or you may care a lot. How much you care will affect the degree of your anger. The more you care, the stronger your feelings of anger may become.

Becky was in tears and couldn't understand why she was so angry with her mother. She felt frustrated and confused and had no idea how to handle the problem. She was a senior in high school, eighteen years-old, and had six more months of living at home. Her parents were divorced, and she no longer spent time with her father. She doubted that she could continue living at home but lacked the financial means to live on her own. She felt trapped. We went for a run together, and she started to discuss her problems. She explained that her anger was so extreme that she found herself staying out late at night to avoid returning home. Her grades were falling and so was her Personal Power; she had lost all sense of control.

We talked about hurt. She felt hurt for many reasons:

- ◊ I'm hurt because I feel that my mom loves my sister more than she loves me. My sister appears perfect in my mother's eyes.
- ◊ I'm hurt because my mom doesn't trust me. She always accuses me of doing bad things. The truth is, I can't think of a single time when I've gotten in serious trouble. I don't understand her lack of trust in me.

We talked about fear. Was there something she was afraid of?

- ◊ I'm scared that my mom doesn't love me anymore. I need her support and the thought of losing her support scares me.

I asked her what she wanted. She didn't say anything for a long time. We ran in silence until she was able to put her thoughts into words:

- ◊ I want to love my mom and be friends with her.
- ◊ I want my mom to love me as I am, not as she thinks I should be.
- ◊ I want to leave for college knowing that I'm always welcome at home.

I asked her if she cared about her mom. She answered very quickly:

- ◊ She's my mom; of course, I care!

I asked her how much she cares about her mom:

- ◊ I care completely because she's my mom.

We went through the list again. I made sure I was clear on everything that she had told me. Then, we talked about caring. The more you care, the more extreme your anger can be if it is misdirected. She was angry because she cared so much.

I asked her what she wanted to do. She said she wasn't sure. She couldn't talk to her mom without getting in a fight. We discussed her options:

- ◊ She could write to her mother explaining her feelings and taking responsibility for her part in the problem.
- ◊ She could ignore her feelings and attempt to graduate and move on with her life.

After considering her options, she decided that writing her feelings was the best solution. She knew she could write her thoughts about love and anger in a non-confrontational way, while expressing her need to have her mom's unconditional love and support.

She wrote the letter and gave it to her mom the following morning. The results were powerful. She finished her senior year, and her mother's pride was obvious at graduation. She went on to college and spends her vacations at home. When I ran into her last Christmas, she was happy, a junior in college, and ready to move forward toward her goal of teaching and coaching soccer.

The building blocks of anger are hurt, fear, desire, and caring. These feelings are driven by how much we care about someone or something. Understanding the emotions behind anger clarifies the problem and helps teenagers make powerful choices.

What can we do about anger? In my work with teens, we spend a lot of time exploring feelings and increasing self-awareness. This work builds to one powerful realization: *you always have a choice*. The key is for teens to take responsibility for their choices. Each choice comes with a unique set of consequences. Understanding and accepting the consequences of one's choices is difficult for anyone, but it is particularly challenging for teens. We spend time working through what it means to make a decision while keeping in mind the possible consequences.

Teens are quick to express their independence. They understand the powerful statement: "No one has control over me; I control my own feelings." Teenagers can develop ways to apply this in positive ways by choosing an alternative to anger.

- ◊ Choose to get away from the situation. Physically leaving is a powerful choice.
- ◊ Realize that being angry is not your only option. There are positive alternatives.
- ◊ Accept responsibility for your choices. Own your words by starting your sentences with "I."
- ◊ Take time to reflect before responding. Remember the old saying, "When you're angry, count to ten before reacting."
- ◊ Talk to yourself, be powerful, and be positive. "No one has the power to make me angry."
- ◊ Talk through the situation with someone you respect and trust.
- ◊ Choose to give yourself some time alone.

Jason entered my classroom and sat on my desk. He was so angry that his entire body was shaking. He was shaking so hard that the items on my desk started to move. I looked up and asked if he needed to talk. Tears started to roll down his cheeks, and he said that he hated his stepfather. He told me that his stepfather had thrown him out of the house the night before. He had stayed with a friend but was still extremely angry.

I asked him if he were hurt. He said, "No, not physically." I asked him if anything else hurt.

- ◊ I'm hurt because my stepfather just wants me out of the house.
- ◊ I'm hurt because my mom married this guy.
- ◊ I'm hurt because, no matter what I say or do, he always blames things on me.

I asked him about his fears. He said he was afraid of many things.

- ◊ I'm afraid that I might have to find somewhere else to live in order to get away from my stepfather.
- ◊ I'm afraid that if I leave home, I might not graduate from high school.

I asked him what he wanted.

- ◊ I want a good relationship with my mom.
- ◊ I want to maintain contact with my dad.
- ◊ I want a better relationship with my stepfather.

I asked him whom he cared about. He responded quickly.

- ◊ I care about my mom.
- ◊ I care about myself.
- ◊ I care about my dad.

He felt that his life had gone downhill since his parents' divorce. He didn't quite understand his emotions, but he knew he loved his mom and he also loved his dad. His only problem was with his stepfather. I asked him what he wanted to do. He went through many ideas: moving out of the house, writing a letter to his mom, living with his dad, ignoring the problem, and attempting to live at home until graduation. He decided to join his mom that evening while she walked the family dog and let her know how he was feeling. They walked together and talked for a long time. His mother was surprised by what he was feeling; yet she understood. She reassured Jason of her love for him. They ended up walking the dog together at least twice a week until he left for college. This helped him gain the security he needed to move on with his life in a powerful manner.

At times, Jason continued to struggle, but his home life became less stressful. He felt proud for taking charge of his feelings and his life. Four years later, he stills spends as much time as possible with his mother. He has open communication with his father and has even grown to appreciate his stepfather. He and his stepfather reached a level of mutual understanding and respect for each other. Jason recently graduated from college and is moving toward his goals and dreams.

If a teenager is angry:

- ◊ They hurt.
- ◊ They fear.
- ◊ They want.
- ◊ THEY CARE.

The more insight teenagers have about their anger, the more likely it is that they will make choices that maintain their integrity and Personal Power.

Seven

Setting Goals For Success

"I bought a journal the other day and I intend to use it all the time. I'm proud of myself because I realize the importance of keeping track of my life and my goals."

Teenagers have the power to create their lives. This power is so strong that what they choose to believe *will* come true. If teenagers choose to create peace and unity in their thoughts, they will find peace and unity in their lives. A teenager creates his or her life by having a vision of where s/he wants to go and setting attainable goals to get there. Teenagers can begin this process by asking themselves three basic questions:

- ◊ Where am I now?
- ◊ Where do I want to be?
- ◊ How am I going to get there?

"He who has a why to live can bear with almost any how."

—Nietzsche

I constantly ask my students, "What is your why? Why did you get up this morning and come to school? Why do you want to graduate? Why do you want to be a success?" When teenagers realize their purpose—the "why" behind their goals—they will find the "how"—the ways to reach their goals. As they think, so they create their view of the world.

In order to succeed, teens must not only set goals but, also, understand the reasons for choosing them. Often the "why" behind a goal is more important than the ultimate result. As teens work to reach their goals, they need to stay focused on their purpose. Goals are not simply about what material things a teen wants to acquire. They are about the type of person they choose to be. I challenge my students to consider what kind of people they want to be and what it will take to become that person.

In Psychology of Success, I ask teenagers to write their goals on the following topics:

- ◊ What are your goals involving family and home life?
- ◊ What are your educational goals?
- ◊ What are your financial goals?
- ◊ What are your career goals?
- ◊ What are your health goals?
- ◊ What are your spiritual goals?

How important is family in their lives? Will they choose to continue to live close to their present home? Why or why not? Do they want to have a family of their own at some point? If so, what is their vision of their family?

Examples of goals that teenagers have shared on family and home:

- "I see myself married and having kids before I'm thirty. I would like to stay in touch with my mom and dad and have my children know my parents. I want my home to be 'homey.' "
- "I'd like to build a house in the woods where I can escape."
- "I'd like to leave home when I graduate, but still have a close relationship with my parents and my sister."
- "I want to create a relationship with my family that is strong enough that we will remain close when I leave. I would like a family in the future, but not for a long time."
- "I want to have a spouse with the same standards I have. I want to have a nice home and raise kids that play sports so I can go and watch them compete. I hope my family and I stay in touch for the rest of my life."
- "I don't have the urge to have a wife and kids. I prefer being by myself."
- "I want to keep in touch with my sister—even though I don't think we'll live in the same town. I want to have a quaint house in a good neighborhood. I see myself with a wonderful man and at least two or three kids that are active in many activities. My kids will be loved and nurtured by their parents."

What are their goals for education? What kind of knowledge do they need? Does their vision include college, a trade school, or going directly into the workforce? What skills do they need to reach their goals?

Examples of educational goals:

- "I see myself studying psychology in Spain and then moving back to the United States to work."

- ◊ "I'd like to ride around on a motorcycle and find people who write books and are willing to share their knowledge with me. I think this would be a great way to learn."
- ◊ "I want to go to college for either theatre or graphic arts, and then do something in either of those two fields."
- ◊ "My main goal is to go to college in Australia. I want to travel and get an education at the same time."
- ◊ "I need to go to a school that focuses on academics. I want to get a wonderful education. I see myself graduating with honors and receiving an acceptance letter to the law school of my choice."

Setting educational goals is an emotional process and can be confusing for teenagers. Teenagers often apply to several colleges and then have a hard time deciding which one to attend. It is important that they make their *own* choices based on what they believe is best for themselves.

John's mother called me on a Sunday afternoon. She explained that John was upset and confused because he had to choose between the University of Colorado and the University of Arizona. She asked if I could speak to him.

I invited John to my house, and we sat on the porch discussing his problem. I invited him to share his reasons for attending the University of Colorado versus the University of Arizona.

He painted a strong argument for Colorado; his brother was attending Colorado. He had been told the academics were better, and he could snowboard and continue living in a winter resort. His list went on and on, but I did not get the sense that Colorado was his dream.

His reason for attending Arizona was because of its great weather, and he could spend so much more time outside enjoying the sun and the warmth. He realized that weather was not a good reason for choosing a college, yet he could not seem to write his name on the Colorado acceptance form.

The problem was clear to me: Colorado was his *head* choice and Arizona was his *heart* choice. I began to ask questions. Isn't choosing a school because of location and weather just as powerful as choosing a school because you think it might have a better academic environment? What is your head saying and what is your heart saying? I invited him to close his eyes and visualize both schools. Which school had a better feel? He said that he felt better when he visualized Arizona, but he still thought he should attend Colorado.

Then I asked him directly, *"Where do you want to attend college?"* Without hesitating he answered, "Arizona." He spent four successful years at the University of Arizona. He recently shared with me that when he arrived on the Arizona campus, he never looked back. He realized his dream and moved in a positive, powerful direction.

I invite students to write down their financial goals in addition to their career goals. What kind of career are they interested in? What are the education and training needs for this career? Will they have to live in a city, or will they be able to work out of their home? Is this a short-term career or a permanent one? How much money do they feel they need? What stage in their lives do they see themselves making the kind of money they need? Some students say they want to be rich, and some just want enough money to take care of their families and to live comfortably. Some students say that money is a low priority, and some believe money will be their driving force.

Examples of financial goals:

- ◊ "I don't need to be rich, but I need enough money for food, warm clothes, a home, the ability to be mobile and travel, a nice camera, and a nice computer. That's all I need."
- ◊ "I don't need much money because money can't buy happiness and I want to be happy."
- ◊ "I want to be able to take a vacation at least once a year. I want to go to the theatre, movies, plays, and dances. I don't want to rely on anyone else for money. I want to be independent."
- ◊ "I want to have enough money to get the things I NEED, but also the things that I WANT."
- ◊ "I'm terrified of not having enough money."
- ◊ "I want to have a lot of money, but I don't want to flaunt it. I want to be able to afford a nice house, a maid, and designer clothes."

I invite students to write down their physical and health goals. Are they athletes that need daily training to stay in shape? Do they love to play on local teams or do they need to train at competitive levels? Do they appreciate their health and realize what it takes to maintain a healthy life? What steps will they take to reach their goals? What are their nutritional needs; will they commit to eating well? Is a healthy lifestyle a priority?

Examples of health goals:

- ◊ "I have always been a healthy eater and I love to exercise. Health is very important to me and I will always be active. There isn't a question of me being out of shape because it just won't happen."
- ◊ "Right now, being in shape is not that important, but I think it will become a goal when I'm older."

- "It's important to run and stay in shape. It is also important to eat healthy foods—but I will *never* give up sweets!"

Setting health goals is different than living the goals they set. Teenagers are not always motivated to live healthy lives.

Alice had written her health goals in her journal during the course Psychology of Success. Being in good shape and eating well were high on her list of life goals. Although she had identified these as her goals, I noticed her lack of energy in class. I also had Alice in aerobics class. Each morning she arrived carrying two chocolate donuts and a soda. I asked about the nutritional content of her chosen breakfast. She knew the breakfast was not good for her, but it seemed to give her energy. I invited her to revisit her health goals and tell me if she thought she was on the path to a healthy life. She grinned and asked if I thought a bagel and orange juice would be a better choice. I returned her smile and invited her to embrace her body and what it needed to remain healthy. I invited her to read her nutritional goals each morning.

I invite students to write down their social goals. How important are people in their lives? Do they enjoy people? Do they see themselves making the world a better place?

Examples of social goals:

- "I love people and I want to be surrounded by everyone. I think I want to live in a city and go out every night."

- "My goal is to live in a small cabin in the woods with my guitar and my books. I will have only a couple of close friends that I will see once in a while."
- "I like people, but I also like to be alone. My goal is to have both in my life—friends *and* privacy."

Teenagers will often live outside their goals and dreams in order to have relationships.

Karen was a people person. She loved to surround herself with friends. Her social calendar was always full. John, her boyfriend, was a quiet, kind person. He loved to watch TV, especially football, and he loved spending time alone with Karen. She came to me in tears because John did not want to take her to the homecoming dance. "What should I do?"

We discussed her options between classes: go to the dance with her friends or stay home and have a quiet evening with John. We discussed the needs and goals of different people. She understood that John was a wonderful person, but maybe he wasn't the right person for her. She needed people in her life, and he seemed happiest when he was alone or with one close friend.

She spoke to John, and he expressed the same frustration she was feeling. He did not like to attend parties or spend time with groups of people. She went to the dance with a group of friends and had a wonderful time. John and Karen became friends and remained friends throughout the year, but never dated again. They were both wonderful and caring teenagers; they just had different social needs and goals.

I invite students to write down their spiritual goals. How important is religion or their chosen spiritual life to them? Oftentimes, my students will remark, "I have no idea, I've never thought about my spiritual goals."

Examples of spiritual goals:

- "My spiritual side is the only thing that really matters to me."
- "I'm not religious or spiritual and probably never will be. I do like being alone and I often spend that time thinking about my life."
- "I care about my spiritual needs. I need something in my life that is bigger than me. Sometimes I need to stop and find out where I'm going and where I've been."
- "I need religion in my life. I need someone to turn to."
- "I need to find my own way of life and my own beliefs."

When teenagers are confused about writing down their goals, I invite them to be completely still for two minutes and take themselves on a journey into their minds, look at the vision of their life and, then, begin to clarify their dreams and goals.

After two minutes, they write down what they envisioned:

- "I see myself living in a beautiful apartment and working as a lawyer. I love my job! I see myself on shopping trips where I buy gorgeous clothes. I see nights on the town dancing and laughing with my friends. I take vacations in exotic places including romantic spots in Europe. I find my soul mate and then have a quaint townhouse in the suburbs with a white fence, a swing, and a garden. I dream of having cute children that run around while I take them to the zoo, Disneyland, and all the places that a child dreams of going."
- "I see myself at San Diego University on a scholarship. I succeed in all of my classes and I am offered a job as in intern in one of the best psychiatric units in the state of California. Two years later, I move to England and work in London. I am offered a great position and I am

making over a million dollars a year. I marry the man of my dreams and have a family while living a wonderful life."

◊ "I see myself attending my dream school. I want to wake up every morning next to my husband who I know loves me more and more every day. My dream is to own and operate a center for eating disorders where young girls can come and get help. I want to help them with their lives. I hope to have children who are eager to learn and enrich their lives. I want to be a good mother giving my children the freedom they need to grow into healthy adults."

Encouraging teens to dream invites purpose into their lives. Dreams come true when teens follow their goals toward their vision. Debbie Ford, author of *The Right Questions,* asks, "Why would anyone take off on a twenty-year journey without a road map?" Teens need a road map for their lives so they can visualize where they are going and how to reach their destination.

Teenage road maps may read like the following:

My road map for the next eight years:
1. Finish high school and receive my diploma.
2. Spend four years studying at a university.
3. Receive my elementary teaching certificate.
4. Apply to teach English in Germany.
5. Move to Germany for three years and teach.
6. Return to the United States and continue my teaching career.

My road map:
1. Graduate from high school.
2. Graduate from college with a bachelor's degree.
3. Get a job in commercial art.

4. Make money so I can live a comfortable life.
5. Travel the world with someone I love.
6. Ski every mountain in the Northwest.
7. Live on a tropical island for one year.
8. When I'm old I want to say, "What an amazing life. I have no regrets."

Goals give teenagers a plan and a purpose to their lives. Step by step by step, reaching goals takes commitment and time. A journey is a gradual process. Teenagers with defined goals will accomplish more than teenagers without goals because goals will guide their behavior and build motivation. It is important for teens to understand the reason for each of their goals. Why do they want to reach each goal and what will they gain?

Examples of goals and reasons why teens want to reach their determined destination:

◊ "I want to study in Madrid during my junior year of college so that I become fluent in Spanish."
◊ "I want to finish my undergraduate degree so I will be accepted into acupuncture school."
◊ "I will not drink alcohol because my family tends to be alcoholics and I never want to be one."
◊ "I will fill out the forms for financial aid because my mom can't help me pay for college."

Teenagers need to set goals that are challenging, but not goals that are impossible. Difficult goals give us satisfaction; impossible goals lead to stress and dissatisfaction.

One student shares his frustration:

> "I promised myself and my parents that I would get an A in algebra. I set a goal and I intend to reach it. I realize that I only have two weeks before the end of the semester and that might be a problem."
>
> "Jess, why do you anticipate a problem? What's your grade right now?"
>
> "I have a 72%—which is a low C."
>
> "Is there the possibility of bringing the 72% up to a 90% in the next two weeks?"
>
> "No, there's only one more test. It's hard material, and I'm a little lost.
>
> "What happens if you give your best and don't receive an A?"
>
> "I know my parents might be disappointed, but in truth I know I did my best. And I will still be proud of my grade."

I encourage teens to have specific goals; vague goals only frustrate them.

Teens share their vague goals and their rewritten specific goals:

> *Vague:* "I would like to build a house in the woods where I can escape."
> *Specific:* "Once I have settled into a job, I will buy a small piece of land on the lake five miles out of town and build a one-room cabin where I can escape from my worries. I want my cabin to be close to where I live so I can separate from my stress quickly and easily."

Vague: "My goal is to apply to college this fall."
Specific: "My college applications will be completed and mailed to the colleges of my choice before Thanksgiving."

Vague: "I need to take the SATs."
Specific: "I have signed up to take the SATs on September 23rd and again on October 17th. I want to make sure I have the option to retake if I don't feel good about my score."

It's important for teens to keep track of their progress toward their goals. In their journals, teens often share how they are doing. Teens are interested in feedback from family, friends, and teachers. Feedback is a way of tracking progress.

A senior football player asked me for feedback on his goal:

"I have a 52% in my writing class, and, if I can't bring it up to 60% in the next week, I won't be allowed to play in the Homecoming game. I don't understand what the teacher is talking about, I'm a terrible writer, and I already know I don't stand a chance."

"Have you talked to your teacher?"

"No, it wouldn't do any good because he doesn't like me."

"I encourage you to meet with your writing teacher and ask for the facts. How can you bring your grade from a 52% to a 60% in the next week? I would love to hear what you learn from your teacher."

He came by my office later that day to follow up with his progress:

"I talked to my teacher, and I was shocked. I'm missing a paper that I wasn't even aware I was missing. He's giving me two days to write the paper and he'll average the points into my present grade. That's not all. He told me that I can take the Friday spelling test on Thursday and he'll also average in that grade. I'm so excited because I know I can do both projects. If I do well, I can play Friday night. Yeah, I am so excited."

I encourage teens to strive for their "personal best." Competing against themselves in working toward a goal will often give them the motivation they need to succeed. Teens don't need to be *the* best—they need to be *their* best.

Teenagers share times when they were competing against themselves:

- ◊ "When I was in treatment for my eating disorder, I competed against myself on a daily basis. I worked on getting better each day. I always wanted to feel better than I had the day before."
- ◊ "I competed against myself on the ACT. I took the test three times just to see if I could get a better score than I received on the previous test. It worked and I improved each time I took the test."
- ◊ "I found the best way to improve my speed on my guitar was to compete against myself. I timed myself every night and felt both joy and frustration depending on how I did."
- ◊ "In order to make the varsity soccer team, we all had to run the mile in a certain time. I ran the mile three times a week and timed myself. I got better and better and easily made the time. I was proud of myself."
- ◊ "I competed with myself throughout the whole track season. Many races I was so far ahead of everyone that I had to set goals for myself so I would continue to improve."

Teenagers who set their own goals are more likely to have the motivation to succeed than if parents, teachers, or coaches set goals for them. The value teenagers place on their goals affects their commitment to the goal. Inviting teenagers to set their own goals is a gift. Through years of experience, I have come to believe that teenagers are the best judges of their own "life journey."

Students write about the differences in goals set by others and goals they set on their own:

1. Goal set by others:

    My parents set a goal that I am supposed to accomplish. The goal is to get straight As. They even offered me $50.00 if I reached *their* goal. No way! I'm barely passing my classes. School is difficult for me and I am working hard just to pass. I have no motivation to get As; it's impossible.

    Goal set by me:

    My goal has always been—and still is—to graduate from high school in four years. I have one more semester and I'll reach my goal. I'm motivated to graduate and I can't wait to receive my diploma.

2. Goal set by others:

    My mom's goal is for me to become a college cheerleader. I don't think I want to cheer in college, but she is pushing me all the time. I'm not motivated to cheer anymore.

    Goal set by me:

    My goal is to get a good score on my SATs so that I can get into the college of my choice. I am working really hard to reach my goal.

3. Goal set by others:

    My coach told me that my goal was to run hard for one entire basketball game. I don't know what he's talking about. I always run hard. I have no motivation to reach this goal because I don't even get it.

Goal set by me:

My goal is to score in double figures in at least half of my games. I'm excited about this goal because I was close last year and I know I can do it this year if I work hard.

Why set goals?

- ◊ Teenagers with goals perform better than teens without goals.
- ◊ Goals guide teenagers in their life journeys.
- ◊ Goals offer a challenge and test self-worth.
- ◊ Goals measure progress.
- ◊ Goals empower teens to control their own destinies.
- ◊ Goals help teenagers find the road to their dreams and live committed, powerful lives.

Eight

Success Is A Teenager Loving Life

"Today has been a great day. Not because something great happened, but just because I want it to be great."

◊ ◊

"A man is what he thinks about all day long."

—Ralph Waldo Emerson

Teenagers' thoughts create their future. Teens need to embrace this concept and understand that they can choose powerful, positive thoughts. Once this is accomplished, they are able to use positive self-talk to move in the direction of their goals and dreams. I invite teenagers to "capture their thoughts" consciously; to become aware of the message behind the thought. Then I ask, "Are your thoughts taking you where you want to go?"

Teenagers write about their thoughts in their journals:

- ◊ "This morning when I woke up, I was thinking about all I need to get done: scholarship applications, training, work, where I'm going to college, what I'm doing after school. I think I'm stressing way too much and that's why I feel overwhelmed."

◊ "When you asked what I was thinking about, I felt good inside. I was thinking about my boyfriend who's going to school in Spain. I was thinking about how much I miss him and how awesome it's going to be when I finally get to see him in December. I also have the song 'Raindrops Keep Fallin' on My Head' stuck in my mind, so I was thinking about that and singing it."

◊ "My thoughts have been powerful today. I was thinking about my friends and how any time I'm not in a good mood, all I have to do is see them in the hall and it automatically puts everything into perspective. Usually the thing I'm upset about isn't even important."

Thoughts are so powerful that what a teen thinks becomes his or her reality. Negative, powerless thoughts can sabotage Personal Power and self-esteem. By consciously choosing positive, powerful thoughts, teens can create a reality that supports their goals and dreams.

"If you think you can, or you think you can't, you're always right."

—Henry Ford

Jamie, a high school junior, walked up to my desk:

"Patzer, I know I'm going to flunk the calculus test. I studied last night, but I know I can't pass."

I asked Jamie if she felt that she had done all she could to prepare for the test.

"Yes, I studied really hard. My dad even helped me."

"Then I believe you will pass. Can you believe that you will pass?"

"I want to believe that, but my thoughts keep telling me that I'll flunk! What can I do?"

"You can consciously change your thoughts. Think: I am prepared and I will pass my test. You own your thoughts. Keep them positive and powerful and you'll be fine. Are you willing to turn your thoughts around?"

Jamie looked me directly in the eye, smiled, and nodded.

The following morning I spoke to her math teacher. He told me she received an 82%. I knew she would be pleased.

You own your thoughts; they do not own you. This is a powerful concept for teenagers to embrace. Once they fully internalize this truth, teens feel a sense of control over the direction of their lives. This sense of control increases their self-esteem and Personal Power.

At first, teenagers may find it difficult to "capture their thoughts," to find the message behind the thought, and understand where their thoughts are leading them. This is often a completely new concept, but with practice they are able to analyze and discuss what they are thinking and how it might affect their journey:

- ◊ "I was thinking about one of my friends that was saying hurtful things about me. It was driving me crazy and I stopped talking to her altogether. These thoughts were not happy thoughts, so I decided that I would help our friendship by changing how I treat her. I'm willing to begin a new type of friendship. I feel good about my new thoughts. I don't feel so angry."
- ◊ "I think everyone who's put on this earth has a reason to be here. It doesn't matter if you're born a genius or not. Everyone has his or her own strengths. I believe everyone should work together to help the

world—and helping is what I want to do with my life. I think my thoughts are powerful and needed in our world."

> "The greatest discovery of my generation is that human beings can alter their lives by altering their attitudes of mind."
>
> —William James

Once teens accept responsibility for their thoughts, they understand that negative thoughts are *just thoughts* and can be changed. Many teens need an invitation to change their thoughts so they can head in a positive direction.

A high school junior wrote to me about taking control of his thoughts:

This soccer season has been quite an experience. I've been feeling pressure from a large number of people in my life. I've been feeling stress from my mom, who's usually optimistic, but now wants me to quit because she doesn't like my coach. I've been feeling stress from my friends because they're tired of hearing how unhappy I am and think I should quit. I've been feeling stress from my coach because I don't think he likes me or wants to deal with me.

I was no longer feeling good about the game or myself. All the negative feelings were affecting my ability to play and enjoy the game. Every day I left practice hating every word that came from the coach's mouth. I started to turn everything he uttered into a negative statement. I would leave practice dreading the next practice. I was so overwhelmed with negative emotions that I felt nothing could go right. It was at this point that I started to share my feelings with you. You invited me to save my season by changing my thoughts. You reminded me that I'm in control of my thoughts and actions. What I realized is that I can't change my coach; I can only change myself. When I spend time thinking about how much I love the game of soccer, a huge difference comes over me. I realize that I'm able to play and enjoy the sport without attaching negative feelings about the coach. I feel so uplifted with my new grasp on the situation that practice is actually fun! I feel something that I have not felt all season long, a <u>positive attitude. I finally want to be positive and not fake that I care about the game, but actually admit that I really *do* care. I'm excited to finish the season!</u>

"The great law simply and briefly stated is that if you think in negative terms, you will get negative results. If you think in positive terms, you will achieve positive results. In three words: believe and succeed."

—Norman Vincent Peale

When teenagers begin to understand the Personal Power inherent in positive self-talk, they quickly become excited about the possibilities of taking control of the direction of their lives. Teenagers are at a point in their lives when they are willing to take risks. When they "risk" changing the way they think, they quickly see the rewards.

High school seniors write:

- ◊ "First I was thinking of my sister who's in jail for drugs. I thought of all the negative aspects of her life. I thought about how ashamed and humiliated I am when people ask where she is. Then I shifted my thoughts to how much I love her and care for her, and how much I want her to get help. Even if I feel embarrassed sometimes, it's OK because she's getting help and that's the most important thing."

- ◊ "My friend likes to put me down by saying negative things about my talents, my other friends, my religion, my attitude, and my family. Her comments are subtle, but hurtful. I started to feel upset, but then I wondered why she was doing it. I think she may feel inferior to me. She can sense my strength and wants to take it down. The more I think about this problem, the more I realize she doesn't have enough positive strength—so she takes it out on me. I decided I could help her gain strength rather than getting mad. It may be hard, but I'll feel better about my friend and myself."
- ◊ "I began by thinking about how I have to give this girl a ride to dance today. I wasn't really looking forward to it because I've never spoken with her and I know she's shy. I hate having awkward moments. To turn this situation into a powerful one, I thought about having the opportunity to get to know her and maybe help her feel more comfortable."

Our minds are constantly crowded with thoughts. Anyone who has studied meditation knows how difficult it can be to empty your mind of thoughts. It is believed that we have an average of 60,000 thoughts per day. How many are positive, how many are negative, and how many are repeated, again and again, throughout the day?

Sometimes our thoughts drift into "daydreams." I often hear a teen say, "I wasn't really thinking about anything. I was thinking about thinking. I looked across at my friend and was wondering what they were thinking."

Daydreams can also take a teen in a positive direction: "When I sat and let my thoughts go through my head, I thought of everyone in my life that I love and how I'm so lucky to have them."

As teenagers learn to redirect negative thoughts, they increase their Personal Power:

- ◊ "I was thinking about how many minutes until the bell rings and I can go home. I was thinking about being hungry and tired and the fact that I didn't want to be in school. When I became aware of my rambling negative thoughts, I decided to change them and see if I felt any different. I started listing my strengths: I'm happy, I'll be successful, I'm beautiful, I love my family, and I'm artistic. Guess what? I honestly did feel better about myself. Changing my thoughts really works! I thought it was crazy, but it's not."

◊ "I've been very stressed lately because all I could think about is where I want to go to college. I couldn't seem to get these thoughts out of my head, so I've been feeling upset. Last night I was talking to my sister, and she helped me work it out by changing the way I thought about it. I realized that no matter where I choose to go, I'd get a good education. Any college or university will be fine. I'm not as stressed about picking the 'perfect' college anymore. What a relief!"

Positive self-talk leads directly to success. Success is teenagers doing what they love. Success is teenagers finding their passion. Success is teenagers heading in the direction of their goals.

When I asked my students to define "success," nearly all related success to personal fulfillment instead of material gains:

◊ "Success is reaching my goals, even when I have to take small steps."
◊ "Success is being happy in what you do and accomplishing your dreams."
◊ "Success is doing what you set your mind and your heart on doing."
◊ "For me, success is being content with my overall life."
◊ "Success is being able to go about doing exactly what I want to do in a positive manner that benefits not only me, but people around me."
◊ "Success is being at a point in life where you are fulfilled and happy."

Successes can be significant events, like graduation from high school, or smaller, daily events like taking care of their little brother to help a parent. Teenagers can experience success on a daily basis. Encouraging teenagers to recognize both their large and small successes helps them to build positive self-esteem and Personal Power.

In Psychology of Success, students write in their journals on a daily basis. When they're asked to list their own personal successes, they write:

- ◊ Last period, I got an 88% on my literature quiz.
- ◊ Last night, I got home late and I still finished my homework.
- ◊ I went to bed early last night.
- ◊ I didn't blow up at my parents for grounding me.
- ◊ I handled myself well in a situation where I could have lost my cool.
- ◊ I successfully said "no" when I needed to.
- ◊ I was nice to my stepfather last night.

A teenager's thoughts create his or her reality. When teenagers have a goal and when they focus their positive self-talk on that goal, they will achieve it!

While running during my lunch hour, I saw a former student walking down the street. Danny had dropped out of school the year before and I had lost contact with him. I stopped to ask how he was doing. He seemed nervous but quickly assured me that he was fine; he was living in town and had a job.

I asked him if he had continued his education, and he told me that he was attending night classes to receive his diploma.

We smiled at each other, said good-bye, and I continued on with my run. When I was about a hundred meters from Danny, I turned and yelled, *"Danny, when you receive your diploma, will you please call me and let me know? I love good news."*

He stopped walking, looked back, and said, "I would love to tell you. I'll call you. Thank you so much. Yes, I'll let you know."

I didn't hear from Danny for another year and four months. One evening, I received a call from him, and he said proudly, "Patzer, I received my diploma."

I knew Danny had experienced the meaning of success.

Positive self-talk leads to success and Personal Power. However, teenagers can have an inner voice that is painful and powerless. In the course Psychology of Success, we refer to this voice as the "negative inner voice." Teenagers' negative voice often undermines their Personal Power by comparing them to others:

- My friend is better looking than I am.
- Dan's parents gave him a car, and I have to buy my own.
- I wish I had been voted best athlete. Sue gets every award.
- My group of friends is popular, but no one likes me.

These comparisons can lead to discontent and jealousy, which decrease self esteem. A teen's negative voice forgets to reinforce his/her strengths and talents but loves to remind him/her of his/her failures. A negative inner voice might even name-call.

- I'm a fatso and I knew I could never stay on that diet. It's no wonder no one likes me.
- Good job, slowpoke. How does it feel to finish dead last?
- I'm so dumb; what made me think I could pass that test?
- Idiot, I can't believe I made such a stupid comment.
- I'm so ugly; I knew no one would like my new outfit.

Teens are capable of changing their thought patterns. The first step is simply becoming aware that thought patterns exist: "I'm being negative, and I need to find a way to break this pattern and think positively." Often a teenager's inner voice is looking for what is wrong instead of what is right. Teenagers have the power to change their negative inner voice to a positive inner voice. This changes how they perceive themselves and everything around them.

A student expresses how she chooses positive thoughts by becoming aware of her negative thought patterns:

- ◊ "I've been feeling so alone. Most of my friends have left for college, and I'm still in high school. Then I think about some of my old friends that are still around and I realize I'm not as alone as I feel. I'm coming back from some hard times, and I know I can make it through this year.
- ◊ "I've also set some personal goals. My goal is to get an A in every class this semester, but I started to doubt if I could do it. Then I thought, 'Why can't I?' I'm smart and I do all my work. I *do* think I can get a 4.0."

Success is a teenager loving life. He or she understands what it takes to be happy and have fun with life. Success is a teen not being afraid to explore new passions and opportunities. Success is when a teenager chooses to "Go for it!" in a positive, powerful way.

Teenagers comment on what it takes to "love their life":

- ◊ "I do love my life. I can truly say that I have a great life. I could write for hours about how many things and great people surround me and support me. I remember lying in my bed at night and just thinking about how great my life is. The other thing that's always a reality check for me is thinking about what my life would be like if I was a starving orphan living on my own. Sometimes I feel weird because I have everything. One of my goals in life is to help feed all of the starving children in the world. I want to help!"

◊ "To truly love my life, I need to live it the way *I* want to. I need to make my own decisions and go with my gut feelings, instead of doing what other people think I should do. I will love my life if I accomplish every goal I set for myself. I want to be happy and really feel like a strong person who doesn't have to rely on others to reach my goals."

When teenagers feel successful, they experience Personal Power. Personal Power is internal confidence.

Personal Power grows when teenagers choose to take **responsibility** for their thoughts, words, and actions. The more responsible teenagers become, the more successful their life will be and the more Personal Power they will possess.

A senior shares her feelings about responsibility:

◊ "I was home alone this weekend for the first time and it went well. I took care of the house and the animals. I was more responsible when my parents were out of town than when they're home. It feels weird to come home to an empty house and do the things my mom usually does. It made me feel in control and mature. I really enjoyed the time that I had to myself. It was relaxing and calming. I did such a good job that my parents told me they'll let me stay home alone next month when they both will be out of town for a meeting. I'm proud of myself."

Personal Power increases as teenagers gain **self-esteem**. When teenagers gain confidence and see the world as positive, their self-esteem increases. When teens choose to live with integrity—when they are honest, trustworthy, and dependable—their self-esteem increases. When teenagers experience self-approval and self-acceptance, when they really love themselves, they experience high levels of self-esteem and Personal Power.

Teenagers write about their self-esteem:

- ◊ "I'm proud of my self-esteem. I'm responsible, caring, and friendly. I'm fun, I'm loving, and I stick to my values."
- ◊ "I see myself as healthy and happy. I also see myself as someone who's always learning. I'm waiting for something and I don't know what it is. I think I'll know what I've been waiting for when it happens."
- ◊ "I'm hardworking, kind, fun, loyal, and dedicated. What worries me is that I think others see me as bland and boring. I don't like that, but I'm proud that I don't see myself as they do."

Personal Power increases as teenagers learn to **care** about themselves as well as others. Personal Power increases when teenagers understand and accept that people have points of view that may differ from their own.

Teenagers write about the way they see others:

- ◊ "The people I most enjoy are strong in spirit. I have a friend who was abandoned by her parents, and she's amazing. Her life is different from mine, but I have such respect for what she's overcome. I enjoy people who set goals and work to accomplish them. These people always look at the positive side and they stay composed and strong in tough situations."
- ◊ "The people I respect are courageous and not judgmental. They are kind and love what they do. I want to be just like that. I care enough about myself to build traits in myself that I respect in others."
- ◊ "I like myself, but I wish I were more confident in my beliefs like so many people I care about are. I wish I never hesitated to say what I believe. I wish I wasn't afraid to talk to other people. I meet people

that have those traits and I tell myself that I can face my fears and learn more about other people and myself. I know it will take time, but I'm willing to do the work."

Personal Power increases as teenagers learn to embrace a **positive attitude**. As teenagers experience their life, they can be taught to choose their attitude—and the attitude they choose can be positive. Negative thoughts may become a habit, so I invite teenagers to recognize their thoughts and change the negative ones to positive thoughts. I've found that teens readily embrace new ways of building a successful, powerful life.

Teenagers can change the negative into the positive by changing the way they perceive an event.

- ◊ "When I had an eating disorder, my life was a negative mess. Then I chose to get help and use my experiences and my knowledge to help others. I went to treatment, bonded with the other girls, and changed my life."
- ◊ "A few years ago, my cousin moved in with our family. She and I did not get along. Most of the year she lived with us felt like a battle. Near the end of the year, we stopped fighting and learned how to live together even if we didn't like each other. When she finally moved away, I was relieved. After she left, I realized that I had learned how to deal with people that I don't like. I can now stay calm when my emotions are running high."
- ◊ "When I was caught shoplifting, I had to spend two nights in a detention center, and that changed my life. Now I look at it as an experience that helped me value my house and my family."

Personal Power increases when a teenager sets goals. Teenagers realize their goals through commitment and perseverance. A teenager with specific goals will accomplish more than a teenager without goals. Goals give teenagers purpose in their lives.

I asked students to share some of their goals:

- Goal: Keep my job for a year.
  It was hard because there were times when I wanted to quit. This was my first real job. I took it one day at a time. The fact that I met my goal surprised even me.
- Goal: I need to pay for an entire trip to Australia by myself.
  I need $1,700 for a plane ticket, and I also need spending money. I worked all summer and have already made $1,900! I bought my plane ticket last week. I am so proud of myself.
- Goal: When I was a little girl, I watched the older dancers on pointe shoes and I told myself I would stay with ballet until I reached that level.
  I accomplished my goal. This spring I will have a lead role in the performance and I will be on pointe.
- Goal: I would not buy another CD until I knew every song on every CD in my collection.
  I used to be a totally impulsive shopper. I love music and I spent all my money on CDs. Since I set my goal, I haven't bought a single CD. It probably sounds crazy, but I am so proud of myself!

I asked teens to describe what Personal Power looks and feels like:

- "If I had tons of Personal Power, I would feel awesome about myself. I would have high self-esteem and be OK with who I am—with how I look, how I act, how well I do in school. I wouldn't care what others thought about me. I would be nice and friendly to everyone, and I would always try to lift others up instead of pulling them down. I would set goals and achieve them. Being powerful is something I want. I want to make a positive difference in my life and other people's lives."
- "If I had Personal Power, I would not only be happy, I would look happy as well. I would say nice things about everyone and banish doubts from my mind."

- ◊ "Personal Power is inner strength that can be seen and felt by others. It's strong, positive energy that fills the heart, mind, and soul. A person with Personal Power has integrity and a strong passion for living life."
- ◊ "Personal Power is understanding who you are and what you want out of life. It is acting powerfully with love, caring, and selflessness. Personal Power is acting the way you want to be treated, also, treating yourself with respect, love, kindness, and truth. People with Personal Power glow; you can tell they're different, confident, and outgoing. You love to be around them."
- ◊ "Personal Power is being responsible for your thoughts, actions, and words. It's understanding that you can't change anyone; you can only invite others to do or see things in a different way. You have confidence, good self-esteem, and are kind to yourself and others. You have a positive outlook on life. You are content."
- ◊ "Personal Power is something that all people have, but may not have discovered. You can recognize Personal Power because it makes you feel confident, worthy of love, and excited about good opportunities. You are proud to be who you are."
- ◊ "I feel my Personal Power is off the Richter scale. I have so much self-confidence and I really do love myself. I believe Personal Power is knowing what you can and cannot do and also realizing that we are all 100% in charge of our lives!"

The Author

Midge Patzer has worked with teenagers for thirty years. She is a public high school teacher, life coach, mentor, and friend to thousands of adolescents across the country. Ms. Patzer has a master's degree in Arts and Humanities and has raised two successful children. Ms. Patzer resides in Sun Valley, Idaho, with her husband and their two dogs.

Ms. Patzer developed her groundbreaking course, *Psychology of Success,* in 1993 as a response to the needs of the many troubled teenagers who were turning to her for help. The course, which focuses on unlocking Personal Power, was an immediate hit and is viewed by many students as their most significant educational learning experience. In 2001 and 2005, she was chosen by the senior class as the graduation keynote speaker and in 2003 Midge was honored with a Presidential Scholars Program Teacher Recognition Award.

Ms. Patzer has focused her professional development on character education, has earned multiple certificates in the field, and teaches private character education seminars and workshops to a variety of audiences throughout the country.